BUILDING AND IMPROVING HEALTH LITERACY IN THE 'NEW NORMAL' OF HEALTH CARE

European Health Management in Transition

Series Editor:

Federico Lega, Full Professor of Health Management and Policy, Director of the Research and Executive Education Center in Health Administration, University of Milan

Books in the series investigate how changes to the health and social care environment are leading to innovative and different practices in health management, health services delivery design, roles and professions, architecture and governance of health systems, patients' engagement and all other paradigmatic shifts taking place in the health context.

The books provide a roadmap for managers, educators, researchers and policymakers to better understand this rapidly developing environment.

Books in the Series:

Federico Lega and Usman Khan: *Health Management 2.0: Meeting the Challenge of 21st-Century Health*

Axel Kaehne and Henk Nies (eds.): *How to Deliver Integrated Care: A Guidebook for Managers*

Federico Lega and Giada Carola Castellini: *Resilient Health Systems: What We Know; What We Should Do*

Federico Lega and Angela Pirino: *Developing and Engaging Clinical Leaders in the 'New Normal' of Hospitals: Why It Matters, How To Do It*

BUILDING AND IMPROVING HEALTH LITERACY IN THE 'NEW NORMAL' OF HEALTH CARE

Frameworks and Actions

BY

FEDERICO LEGA
University of Milan, Italy

And

PIA KREUTZER
Medical University of Vienna, Austria

United Kingdom – North America – Japan – India
Malaysia – China

Emerald Publishing Limited
Howard House, Wagon Lane, Bingley BD16 1WA, UK

First edition 2023

Reprints and permissions service
Contact: permissions@emeraldinsight.com

British Library Cataloguing in Publication Data
A catalogue record for this book is available from the British Library

ISBN: 978-1-83753-339-8 (Print)
ISBN: 978-1-83753-336-7 (Online)
ISBN: 978-1-83753-338-1 (Epub)

ISOQAR certified
Management System,
awarded to Emerald
for adherence to
Environmental
standard
ISO 14001:2004.

Certificate Number 1985
ISO 14001

INVESTOR IN PEOPLE

This book is dedicated to all the passionate and dedicated health workers and health managers that make our lives safer and better.

CONTENTS

ABBREVIATIONS

AI	Artificial Intelligence
AT	Austria
BG	Bulgaria
CVD	Cardiovascular Disease
CY	Republic of Cyprus
CZ	Czech Republic
DE	Germany
DK	Denmark
EBM	Evidence-Based Medicine
EE	Estonia
EHL	eHealth Literacy/Electronic Health Literacy
EL	Greece
ES	Spain
EU	European Union
FI	Finland
FR	France
HL	Health Literacy
HR	Croatia
HU	Hungary
IE	Ireland
IT	Italy
LE	Life Expectancy
LT	Lithuania
LU	Luxembourg
LV	Latvia
MOOC	Massive Open Online Course
MT	Malta
NCD	Non-Communicable Disease
NL	The Netherlands
OHC	Online Health Community
PCL	Patient-Centred Medication Labelling
PL	Poland

PP	Patient Portal
PSG	Patient Support Group
PT	Portugal
REALM	Rapid Estimate of Health Literacy in Medicine
RO	Romania
SE	Sweden
SI	Slovenia
SILS	Single Item Literacy Screener
SK	Slovakia
TOFHLA	Test of Functional Health Literacy in Adults
UK	United Kingdom
US	United States
WHO	World Health Organization

ABOUT THE AUTHORS

Federico Lega, PhD, is Full Professor of Health Policy, Management and Economics at Milan University and Director of the Research Center in Health Administration (HEAD). He's the past President of EHMA and chair of its scientific advisory committee and the current Editor-in-Chief of the journal *Health Services Management Research*. He regularly advises health systems, organisations and life science industries. He has published over 10 books and 150 journal articles.

Pia Kreutzer is a double-degree graduate of the Vienna University of Economics and Business (Strategy, Innovation and Management Control) and Bocconi University (Economics and Management of Innovation and Technology). She is especially passionate about the intersection of Medicine and Business/Economics which is why she is currently pursuing her MD at the Medical University of Vienna.

1

HEALTH LITERACY AS A KEY FACTOR IN THE 'NEW NORMAL' OF HEALTH CARE SYSTEMS

Health literacy is a stronger predictor of an individual's health status than income, employment status, education, and racial or ethnic group.
                                    –World Health Organization

Literacy is a bridge from misery to hope...
                                    –Kofi Annan

'Health literacy is linked to literacy and entails people's knowledge, motivation and competences to access, understand, appraise and apply health information in order to make judgements and take decisions in everyday life concerning health care, disease prevention and health promotion to maintain or improve quality of life during the life course' (Sørensen et al., 2012, p. 83). This definition by the World Health Organization (WHO) is used throughout this book.

But why is health literacy (HL) important? Studied for decades, health literacy research has reached consensus on certain aspects. First, health literacy is a vital life skill for individuals. Health care in general, and primary care in particular, have begun to adopt a patient-centred approach that empowers patients, helps to co-create and co-produce health services and co-create value. To do this, greater health literacy is essential. Second, health literacy is a public health imperative. As population health has gained wider attention, so, too, primary care and preventive medicine have gained importance. Nevertheless, many population health initiatives expect that people understand their circumstances, for which health literacy is a prerequisite. Third, health literacy is an integral part of social capital and indispensable for reducing health inequalities (Washington et al., 2018). Finally, it is also an economic issue. While low health literacy has been linked with underutilisation of health services and underdiagnosis, research has also revealed potential overutilisation of health services and overdiagnosis (Jessup & Buchbinder, 2018). Low health literacy has been associated with greater disease burden and worse health outcomes that absorb health care system resources (Kickbusch et al., 2006).

In brief, health literacy should be a top priority on the agenda of any health policy/system/agency. Here we argue that health literacy is a key element in building effective, sustainable and resilient health services. To better understand this point, we first need to examine the context of the 'new normal' in health care and its provision.

There is no academic definition of the 'new normal' in health care; however, it is very clear to practitioners when they realise that:

- the social media have gained pervasive influence on health and medical information (often misinformation)

- there is a need to co-produce and co-create health services with patients and caregivers who possess an adequate level of health literacy

- public agencies often fail to provide public health services and health education due to funding cuts (COVID-19 has demonstrated the effects)

- immigration has far-reaching consequences for public health/health behaviours

- young people are adopting unhealthy/risky habits (tobacco, alcohol and drug use)

- there is a need to better coordinate social and health care services for an ageing population with chronic conditions

- that there are limited financial resources

- patients expect to be informed, involved and treated as clients

Health care has become complex. The current dynamics are not conjunctural but rather structural. ... As such, they define the 'new normal'. A taxonomy of the changes characterising the 'new normal' in the health sector describes two clusters of structural change. The one concerns current developments, i.e. challenges due to:

1. Shifts in epidemiology

- an ageing population with differentiated care needs

- frail patients (chronic, frequent service users, not self-sufficient) need an integrated continuum of care

- highly dependent, critical patients may not be so unstable as to require intensive care but rather an advanced care setting

- post-acute surgical patients need medical attention and integrated follow-up

- elderly patients with cognitive problems, complex social backgrounds

2. Technical and technological innovations in service delivery

   - freestanding surgery, mini-invasive techniques, robotics and procedures (e.g. day surgery, one-day surgery, week surgery) require greater self-care by patients

   - increased risk of turf wars due to the overlapping between areas in medical, surgical and interventional diagnostics (cardiovascular, neuroscience, oncology)

3. Expectations of improved flow and quality of care

   - building patient-centred hospitals designed around patient needs

   - greater efficiency and productivity, and specific pathways for urgent and elective care

   - multidisciplinary teamwork

4. Outcome accountability

   - tracked attention to evidence-based medicine and clinical governance

   - patient-reported experience measures and patient-reported outcome measures (PREMs and PROMs) taken into account, with a greater role for patients

These challenges make up only a subset of what health care managers really handle. The second cluster comprises the reasons why health care is so complex and health care organisations so challenging to manage: a prototype of the volatile, uncertain, complex ambiguous (VUCA) environment.

Health care systems are entering a new normality not merely in the ways they evolve but how revolution can drastically change them. Disruptive innovation is fast and furious: artificial intelligence, robots, precision medicine, regenerative medicine. Technology and algorithms are set to govern health care procedures. Financial struggles are common to all countries, even the richest. In many places, health care professionals are facing a loss in status and role, and there is a widespread shortage of doctors in many developed and developing countries. New business models for low-cost or low-price health care, focussed hospitals and medical tourism have entered the health care marketplace.

In this evolving and revolutionary context, new paradigms are needed to cope with this new normality. A paradigm shift that can increase the chance to meet quality and sustainability challenges.

One major effort is to implement the logic of population health management. This implies managing health and wellness proactively, with a focus on prevention, risk factor reduction and management of chronic conditions, while supporting the co-creation and co-production of health care services. Health literacy regards not only individuals concerned with their own or their family's health but also organisations, public health systems and society as a whole. Bitzer and Sørensen (2018) argue, for example, that systems, institutions and other health organisations must be 'responsive', i.e. they must provide health information, resources, support and environments in such a way that they are equally accessible and useable by people with different levels of health literacy. The societal importance of health literacy concerns prevention and adequate treatment. Since a health literate person is more likely to maintain good health status, primary prevention is involved. But health literacy is also vital in secondary prevention. Ratzan and Parker (2000) mention that ineffective communication between health care providers and patients could cause medical errors due to misunderstanding or misinformation about treatment and self-care instructions.

In this light, fostering health literacy poses a challenge for patients and health systems and organisations alike. If we really want to change the dominant paradigm in care provision from compliance to concordance (where the health care professional and the patient build an alliance with one another), and from empowerment to self-management and co-production, we will need to raise the level of health literacy across the population. Investment in health literacy brings returns, since quality, efficacy and sustainability have a positive correlation with co-production and concordance. Furthermore, better informed patients may be more difficult to manage and keener to spot and assess deficiencies in health care delivery. Ultimately, such health-user pressure could push health care systems and professionals towards a patient-centred organisation that is expected and desired.

Moreover, population health management is often linked to the Triple Aim notion: an approach developed by the Institute for Healthcare Improvement (IHI) to optimise health system performance (Berwick et al., 2008). According to the IHI, the goal of the Triple Aim is to 'improve the patient care experience, improve the health of a population, and reduce per capita health care costs'. It is a single strategy with three key goals.

The recently introduced fourth goal – to improve clinical experience – has led to the creation of the Quadruple Aim (Bodenheimer & Sinsky, 2014). The idea is that, without an improved clinical experience on the provider side, the three other patient-centric aspects won't reach their full potential. The four components of this framework, around which all

European countries are developing (or should develop) their current strategic directions of health policy, are:

1. Improved patient experience. Improving the patient experience aims to enhance the quality of care that patients receive, with a greater focus on individuals and their families. The focus is on safety, effectiveness, patient-centredness, timeliness, efficiency and equity. This means adopting the logics of business modelling in health care to design service delivery. Plus, attention is devoted to health literacy, as more educated patients can be expected to manage their health more effectively.

2. Better Outcomes. With the Triple Aim comes the goal of improving the health of the overall population by measuring outcomes, increasing transparency and incentivising by pay-for-performance.

3. Lower Costs. The Triple Aim intends to reduce the per capita cost of health care. Keeping this aspect linked to improved patient experience and improving the health of populations ensures that when costs are driven down, the quality of care isn't diminished.

4. Improved Clinical Experience. The aim is to create conditions and motivation for the most effective delivery of health services. It's the responsibility of managers. The pressure on caregivers is immense, leading to unwanted outcomes that can reduce the quality of the care they provide. Research has shown a correlation between low staff engagement and burnout and low patient satisfaction, poor health outcomes and high costs – which contrast the Triple Aim approach. To combat this, an improved clinical experience should be included in the Triple Aim, updating it to the Quadruple Aim. The Quadruple Aim is the

framework that guides the direction that health care systems – including patients and providers – should pursue. As Rome was not built in a day, the change will not happen overnight nor will improvement in health care system performance. It's a long-term objective that can be reached through short-term goals (and objectives) set by single providers and agencies.

Several issues need to be addressed by health policymakers and managers. If patients are at the centre, how can the shift from compliance to concordance be made? How can the co-creation and the co-production of services be developed? Empowerment entails not only qualification but also engagement and co-responsibility. Chronic care models are evolving in population health care management. But what exactly is happening? Attention should be directed towards risk factors and prevention. How can this be organised? How can individuals be more informed of their risk factors and lifestyles?

There are many questions and challenges but few certainties. One of which is that health literacy is fundamental for health systems to meet the changes ahead and adopt to new paradigm shifts. There are myriad reasons why we should care about health literacy. But before discussing each in more detail, we first need to understand what we mean when we talk about health literacy. We will then situate health literacy in the context of the 'new normal' of health care and its implications.

The next chapter (Chapter 2) gives a short history and background of health literacy, followed by definitions (Chapter 3). The relevance and correlations of health literacy are then analysed and the methods to assess and measure it.

Finally, health literacy will be contextualised in the 'new normal' and interventions to improve it will be outlined, as well as the tools to sustain its improvement, such as clinical pathways.

The Conclusions will focus on how to 'make things happen' and the implications for health policymakers and managers. The appendix lists the data and references to the research protocol for writing this book.

2

HEALTH LITERACY: DEFINITION AND BACKGROUND

2.1 BRIEF HISTORY AND BACKGROUND OF THE CONCEPT OF HEALTH LITERACY

In order to adequately place the concept of health literacy within the 'new normal' of health care, it makes sense to examine its history. First used by Simonds in 1974 in a paper titled 'Health education as social policy' (Simonds, 1974), he asked for minimal standards for health literacy at all school grade levels in health education as a policy involving the health care system, the educational system and mass communication. Starting from this health education basis, health literacy gained clinical relevance in the 1990s, when it was understood as a patient's ability to understand medical instructions, package leaflets and patient information. It was seen as a part of general literacy, i.e. the ability to read, write and possess basic numerical skills in a medical context. In 1998 the concept was gradually extended beyond basic cognitive capabilities (so-called functional health literacy) to a wider range of skills in finding medical information from various different sources, evaluating the information and applying it to one's personal situation, as well as to communicate relevant information (e.g. in conversation with one's physician; now termed interactive/communicative health literacy) and to distinguish between and critically appraise health issues (now called critical health literacy) (Bitzer & Sørensen, 2018).

For some years, there has been a shift from educating only medical students to educating the general public with the aim to improve or maintain population health. Notions of patient-centricity and medical advances opening new therapeutic options and documentation that medical errors account for one-third of the cause of adult deaths in the United States have led to a reform in patient education. Patients are expected to assume more responsibility for their health as full members of their own health care team (Dirmaier & Härter, 2011; Weinstein et al., 2017). In assuming this role, they contribute by seeking the information that they need (e.g. on the internet, where health care information has become more easily accessible), and ethical considerations, medical legislation, as well as scientific findings of the implications.

The role of health care professionals has also evolved, making health literacy among patients a prerequisite (Hämeen-Anttila, 2016) for navigating 'the new normal' and complex, fragmented health care systems, where patients are expected to self-care and seek health care, especially for chronic conditions (Hersh et al., 2015).

2.2 IN SEARCH OF A DEFINITION (AND TAXONOMY)

Health literacy is variously defined and interpreted by its implications for the delivery of care and health care services, as well as for policies and initiatives (Malloy-Weir et al., 2016). The historical development of what health literacy means may also be traced in some of its former definitions.

One of the most widely used definitions of health literacy states that it 'is the degree to which individuals have the capacity to obtain, process, and understand basic health information and services' (Ratzan & Parker, 2000, p. vi). Ratzan and Parker (2000) add that a variety of skills (e.g. writing, numeracy, communication and new technologies) is necessary to undertake such tasks successfully and confidently navigate a health care system. This definition was also employed by researchers who followed Ratzan and Parker's example, such as Marshall et al. (2012), and with adaptations by Caruso et al. (2018).

Kickbusch et al. (2006, p. 4) define health literacy as 'the ability to make sound health decisions in the context of everyday life – at home, in the community, at the workplace, in the health care system, the market place and the political arena. It is a critical empowerment strategy to increase people's control over their health, their ability to seek out information and their ability to take responsibility'. While this definition has been broadened and a particular skill set added, it does not explicitly state which skills are actually needed.

In 2012 the European Health Literacy Consortium agreed on a definition that would encompass all previous definitions of major importance: 'Health literacy is linked to literacy and entails people's knowledge, motivation and competences to access, understand, appraise, and apply health information in order to make judgments and take decisions in everyday life concerning healthcare, disease prevention and health promotion to maintain or improve quality of life during the life course' (Sørensen et al., 2012, p. 83). This is also the definition that the WHO adopted (WHO, 2013) in a more recent publication (WHO Health Evidence Network, 2019). The latter states a similar version: 'Health literacy can be defined as the capacity of individuals, families and communities to access, understand, appraise and apply health information in order to make judgements and take decisions in everyday life concerning health care, disease prevention and health promotion in order to maintain or improve their quality of life' (WHO Health Evidence Network, 2019, p. viii). In the former definition, a person's willingness was included, and the broader skill sets and the actual implementation of information were acknowledged as facets. Furthermore, the definition incorporated the current concept of quality of life. In the latter, one could argue that 'knowledge, motivation and competences' were subsumed under the umbrella of 'capacity'. 'People', on the other hand, was defined more precisely by breaking it down into 'individuals, families and communities'. Widening the focus from individuals to communities has signalled a progression that scholars have mentioned (Rogers et al., 2014). The definition by Sørensen et al. (2012) will be used in this book.

Bitzer and Sørensen (2018) analysed the use of health literacy and identified four steps:

1. Being able to seek, find and gain access to relevant health information. The information may be accessed through written material, such as pamphlets and websites, but it could also encompass contact and communication with counselling centres, self-help services, medical professionals or outpatient centres.

2. Understanding the information and grasping its content. Here, the skills of reading comprehension, textual and numeracy understanding come into play.

3. Assessing the information, which comprises the capability to interpret what was communicated, filter what is relevant, and evaluate its reliability and quality.

4. The acquired information must be implemented, and necessary steps taken and communicated. Therefore, (informed) decisions must be taken (for oneself or a relative) to maintain or improve one's health and, possibly, convey it to a health care provider.

Besides these four steps, others such as the motivation to undertake them, the willingness and intent to assume responsibility, assertiveness, and the capability to utilise (social) resources and to navigate the health care system are also important (Bitzer & Sørensen, 2018). Health literacy does not only necessarily determine one's own health and actions but also that of target audiences (e.g. children) that are oftentimes influenced by their social and political surroundings. Through parents, family members, friends and political representatives, an individual's level of health literacy has an impact on personal circumstances (Bitzer & Sørensen, 2018). Bitzer and Sørensen (2018) continue that individual health literacy is to be interpreted as a dynamic concept. If the external circumstances (e.g. the legal framework, the supply of certain health products or services) or the individual situation (e.g. migration or new health issues) change, it may be vital to adapt or expand one's health literacy or to acquire new skills and knowledge. Health literacy skills may vary within an individual; over time, they may be impacted by emotional states, acute pain or illness, vision and hearing deficits, and cognitive impairment (Baker et al., 2000).

Below are three more perspectives on health literacy that complete a taxonomy for distinguishing the various different approaches to its study.

2.2.1 Individual Health Literacy

Nutbeam (2000) differentiated three different levels: functional, interactive or communicative, and critical health literacy. Functional health literacy refers to the basic skills of daily life, such as reading and writing, while interactive or communicative health literacy comprises cognitive skills and literacy, and critical health literacy refers to adequate decision-making within a health care system. This three-tiered distinction offers a helpful guide to where potential problems may arise. However, it may also have limitations on how to measure each sub-category or if all potential issues are covered and fall into one of the categories exclusively. In their study, Bowskill and Garner (2012) focussed on functional health literacy.

While health literacy plays a critical role in all medical specialities, many studies have focussed on one of the specific interests, such as mental health literacy (Amarasuriya et al., 2015; Attygalle et al., 2017; Pinto-Meza et al., 2013; Umubyeyi et al., 2016). In their naturalistic study, Goldney and Fisher (2008, p. 129) define mental health literacy as 'the knowledge and beliefs about mental disorders that aid in their recognition, management, or prevention; it is also a determinant of help seeking'.

Another frequent differentiation in research is whether (potential) patients or their family members exhibit a certain level of health literacy and whether health care providers can react to the level of health literacy of the person they are dealing with. Assessment and action by health care professionals may dramatically influence how a patient will be able to assimilate the information they are being given. This prerequisite to providing people with an adequate level of information enables them to take part in managing their own health care. A patient-centred system of care that allows co-production and co-creation is indispensable to fully exploit one's health literacy (Bitzer & Sørensen, 2018).

Another concept that is gaining attention is digital health literacy or electronic health literacy or eHealth literacy. Such approaches apply health literacy to digital and electronic devices for communication and are used synonymously. A widely used definition for digital health literacy states that digital health literacy (or eHealth literacy, EHL) is 'the ability to seek, find, understand, and appraise health information from electronic sources and apply the knowledge gained to addressing or solving a health problem' (Norman & Skinner, 2006b, p. 1). The growing popularity of the internet and other online sources of health information was noted by Parker et al. (1995). Examples of digital/electronic health literacy are discussed in Section 5.2.

2.2.2 Public Health Perspective

Rogers et al. (2014) argue that given the rapidly rising prevalence of non-communicable diseases such as diabetes, especially among minority and low-income youth, it is critical to move the conversation from individual behaviour more towards a socio-ecological perspective, in which they apply a public-health literacy framework.

2.2.3 Organisational Health Literacy

Palumbo (2021, p. 115) defines another sub-category of health literacy. 'Organizational health literacy involves the health care organizations' ability to establish an empowering and co-creating relationship with patients, engaging them in the design and delivery of health services in collaboration with health professionals'. Research indicates that organisational health literacy contributes to health promotion and risk prevention by adopting a patient-centred approach to care and patient empowerment, thus playing a vital role in the overall picture of health literacy.

3

HEALTH LITERACY MEASUREMENT, ASSESSMENT AND ASSOCIATION

There are many good reasons why the general public and public health agencies should work towards improving health literacy: it is an essential skill for individuals, a crucial public health issue, and a vital part of social capital and the economy. The following sections discuss the measurement, assessment and association of health literacy.

3.1 HOW HEALTH LITERACY CAN BE SYSTEMATICALLY ASSESSED AND MEASURED

This section gives an overview of instruments commonly used to assess health literacy. These tools were most frequently retrieved by our literature research. Readers are referred to Pleasant et al. (2019) for a more detailed discussion of measurement tools.

3.1.1 Single Item Literacy Screener

The Single Item Literacy Screener (SILS) is a simple instrument to determine whether a person has adequate or limited reading abilities, in which case support when reading health information is required (Morris et al., 2006). The item asks: 'How often do you need to have someone help you when you read instructions, pamphlets, or other written material from your doctor or pharmacy?'; and the responses are (1) Never, (2) Rarely, (3) Sometimes, (4) Often and (5) Always.

3.1.2 Test of Functional Health Literacy in Adults

The Test of Functional Health Literacy in Adults (TOFHLA) is an objective test of knowledge and numeracy. The long version consists of 67 items and the short version 36 items; the twenty-two- or seven-minute timed instrument tests reading comprehension. Results are categorised as inadequate, marginal or adequate health literacy (Morris et al., 2006; Okan et al., 2019; Pleasant et al., 2019).

3.1.3 Rapid Estimate of Health Literacy in Medicine

The Rapid Estimate of Health Literacy in Medicine (REALM) is a test-based assessment that only takes a few minutes to administer. The patient is asked to read a list of words out loud. It provides an approximate assessment of reading ability (Hersh et al., 2015; WHO Health Evidence Network, 2019).

3.1.4 European Health Literacy Survey Questionnaire

The European Health Literacy Survey Questionnaire (HLS-EU) is a self-reported survey tool. The original version (HLS-EU-Q86) was composed of 86 items; shorter versions have 47 items (HLS-EU-Q47) or 16 items (HLS-EU-Q16) and results are categorised as excellent, sufficient, problematic and inadequate health literacy (Pleasant et al., 2019; Pelikan et al., 2019). A detailed description of this tool is given in Pelikan et al. (2019).

3.1.5 eHealth Literacy Scale

The eHealth Literacy Scale (eHEALS) is one of the very few validated, self-reported tools for assessing eHealth literacy. It comprises eight items (Norman & Skinner, 2006a). According to Pleasant et al. (2019), it is the only eHealth measurement tool that has been applied in different settings globally.

3.1.6 Ad hoc Assessment by Medical Professionals

How medical professionals assess the health literacy of their patients is crucial for determining their interaction (see Section 3.1). This plays an enormous role in people's understanding.

In their study, Vargas et al. (2014) evaluated plastic surgeons' assessment of their patients' literacy and found that about 62% of surgeons assessed their patients based on general impression, while about 37% asked their patients about their employment and used that as an assessment criterion. About 26% stated that they did not assess health literacy. In general, plastic surgeons overestimated both the level of education and the reading level of their patients compared with national data, which may be problematic for how to handle their patients' communication needs.

Wilson et al. (2018) examined patient-centred discharge planning, which aims to improve transitional care and outcomes of vulnerable adults. The initiative involved internal medicine residents visiting recently discharged patients during inpatient rotations and addressed patients' shortcomings in understanding, rectifying medication errors and providing health education. The interns reported major increases in their patient-centred discharge planning skills and providing culturally sensitive health services. They also improved their communication skills, eliciting patient illness narratives, assessing patient safety, functional status and health literacy more effectively (Wilson et al., 2018).

3.2 STATE OF THE ART: OVERVIEW OF HEALTH LITERACY ASSESSMENT IN EUROPE

The following data are derived from a European health literacy survey (Sørensen et al., 2015) that applied the HLS-EU tool (see Section 3.1). Mean health literacy scores varied widely between countries, with a difference of 6.56 points between the Netherlands and Bulgaria, the two countries with the highest (37.06) and the lowest (30.50) mean score, respectively (out of a maximum score of 50). In the total sample, 12.4% had inadequate health literacy, and almost every second respondent (47.6%) had limited health literacy, i.e. inadequate or problematic health literacy (Sørensen et al., 2015) (Fig. 1).

Readers are referred to Sørensen et al. (2015) for a discussion of how these results were obtained and for a further analysis.

The Flash Eurobarometer 404 (European Union, 2014a) gives an overview of people's use of the internet for health information: 59% of respondents stated they used the internet to search for health-related information within the last 12 months, 32% reported doing so at least once a month. The most frequently sought information was 'on lifestyle choices, such as diet, nutrition, physical activity, smoking, alcohol, etc.' Some 74% of respondents stated they had used the

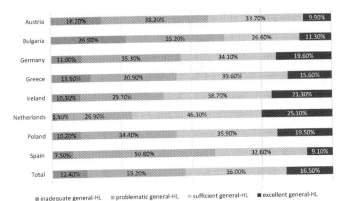

| | inadequate general-HL | problematic general-HL | sufficient general-HL | excellent general-HL |

Source: Adapted from Sørensen et al. (2015), plotted by the authors.

Fig. 1. Levels of General Health Literacy (HL) Index.

internet to search for health-related information and 89% stated they were satisfied with the health-related information they found, with the majority being 'fairly satisfied'. When those who were not satisfied were asked for their reasons as to why, most said that the information was not reliable. The feeling that the information was commercially oriented was the second most common reason, while the third most common was that the information was not detailed enough. Nonetheless, 77% agreed with the statement that 'the internet is a good tool to help improve my knowledge of health-related topics' (European Union, 2014b, 2014a). These beliefs and opinions underline the importance of eHealth literacy. People seem eager and willing to improve their health literacy through the internet, but before they can take full advantage of the benefits, they need to be digitally health literate.

3.3 FURTHER ANALYSIS

We conducted an analysis to assess the association between health literacy and health system performance. A qualitative approach was applied to examine the role of health literacy within the 'new normal' of health care. A systematic review of the literature was conducted to analyse the interaction between these two concepts. Several health literacy interventions and initiatives were investigated, with a focus on the potential of new technologies to enhance health literacy. Building on the findings, implications and lessons for policymakers and health care managers will be presented in later sections of this volume.

3.3.1 Systematic Review

We conducted a systematic literature review to determine the relevance of health literacy in the context of the 'new normal' of health care, or more precisely, in reference to population health management, initiative medicine, co-production and co-creation of value. We searched the electronic database PubMed using the terms 'health literacy' AND 'population health management' OR 'initiative medicine' OR 'medicine of initiative' OR 'co-production of health' OR 'co-production' OR 'co-creation' OR 'co-creation'. The search retrieved 243 records, three of which were duplicates, thus yielding 240 records for screening. The results are given as a narrative literature review. The publications are listed in the Appendix (Annex A).

3.4 RELEVANCE: IMPACT ON EQUITY AND ACCESSIBILITY. ASSOCIATION WITH DEMOGRAPHIC, SOCIO-ECONOMIC AND HEALTH FACTORS

In their study, Levy and Janke reported that low health literacy was, on average, associated with a lower education level, a greater likelihood of belonging to a racial or ethnic minority, poor health and a greater likelihood of cognitive impairment (Levy & Janke, 2016). They also found that individuals with low health literacy were also highly likely to be older. In contrast, in their study involving college students, Rababah et al. (2019) stated that this association disappeared in univariate and follow-up analyses. Nonetheless, the much smaller age difference among college students than among the general public might have influenced their findings. Also, male gender has been associated with lower performance on some variables of health literacy (Emmerton et al., 2012).

Since health information has become more easily accessible, people play a much more active and autonomous role in managing their health while navigating the vast amounts of health information on their own. Critical appraisal of the information can prove difficult due to the lack of regulation and the questionable quality of sources. Without the knowledge and skills to evaluate completeness and accuracy of the information, which are central to health literacy, people can make ill-informed health choices. Health literacy serves to counteract such mistakes. There is a positive association between health literacy and better knowledge about diabetes, for example, according to Marciano et al. (2019).

People with low health literacy may find it difficult to process new information about disease management (e.g. reading appointment slips or drug labels), or to understand what their health care provider or other educational material is explaining (Mayeaux et al., 1996; Schillinger et al., 2002). There is also evidence for an association between low health literacy and poorer health care–related knowledge (Gazmararian et al., 2003; Kalichman et al., 2000; Williams et al., 1998b, 1995), lower medication adherence (Kalichman et al., 2000; Persell et al., 2007; Williams et al., 1998a), underuse of prevention services (Fathy et al., 2016; Scott et al., 2002), poorer physical and mental health (Baker et al., 1997; Wolf et al., 2005), increased hospitalisation rates (Baker et al., 1998) and reduced patient safety (Hersh et al., 2015).

Aaby et al. (2020) found that health literacy could be a crucial aspect in initiatives seeking to improve participation in and outcomes of interventions. Johri et al. (2015) found a positive association between maternal health literacy and child vaccination rates. In general, children of parents with higher levels of health literacy are more likely to achieve better outcomes in child health promotion and disease prevention (Sanders et al., 2009). Levy and Janke (2016) reported that there is little empirical evidence sustaining the belief that people with low health literacy have less access to health care. They went on to argue that the reason may be that many studies, due to their design, underestimate the negative association between low health literacy and access to health care because study samples frequently involve individuals who already have a health care provider or access to a health care system and find no obstacles to obtaining their health care. Of note, however, is that individuals with low health literacy may delay seeking care due to cost or other reasons and report that they often had difficulty finding a health care provider (Levy & Janke, 2016). For a deeper analysis of access to health care and the reasons behind delaying care, see Levy and Janke (2016).

Attygalle et al. (2017) have found that mental health literacy improves help-seeking strategies, which is known to be poor in adolescents. Wang et al. (2007) found that high health literacy may be one of the promising ways to reduce the stigma associated with depression. Health literacy is an essential skill for chronic disease management and achieving favourable health outcomes and quality of life (Bailey et al., 2014; Green et al., 2013; Matsuoka et al., 2016; McNaughton et al., 2014).

In their study, Marciano et al. (2019) reported that the more patients are in need (e.g. due to lower education level and lack of health insurance), the stronger the association between health literacy and target blood glucose levels, as measured by glycated haemoglobin A1C, a vital health outcome in diabetes care. They suggested that general education and health insurance may help patients to stay within the target range, while the value of health literacy is to obtain desirable health outcomes.

Health literacy has also been shown to be a partial mediator of racial and ethnic disparities in asthma knowledge and asthma-related quality of life, and may help to reduce disparities in health outcomes (Washington et al., 2018). Matima et al. (2018) argued that the burden of self-care may vary in difficulty according to such capacity factors as positive attitudes, optimal health literacy, social support and the availability of economic resources. Readers are referred to Dowrick et al. (2013) for an in-depth analysis of potential barriers and facilitators of access to evidence-based health services and interventions acceptable to currently underserved groups.

3.5 RELEVANCE: IMPACT ON SUSTAINABILITY AND ASSOCIATION WITH ECONOMIC FACTORS

While economic factors are beyond the scope of this book, the literature search retrieved several studies that found an association between health literacy and economic status. Low health literacy has been found to be a major risk factor for not having health insurance (Levy & Janke, 2016; Sentell, 2012). Rababah et al. (2019) reported that low health literacy raises health care costs. Betz et al. (2008) shared this observation that low health literacy is a causative factor of increased health care costs. In addition to the health problems that inadequate treatment may bring about, over- or under-utilisation of health services may result in a higher burden of disease and higher treatment costs. Under-utilisation might allow a condition to become more severe or difficult to treat before being diagnosed. Behnke et al. (2013) stated that shared decision-making may be helpful to address inadequate over-utilisation and that assessing patients for health literacy could aid in doing so.

Also other factors associated with health literacy such as hospitalisation, medication adherence, lack of preventive services or diagnostic testing and health monitoring (Akter et al., 2014; Fathy et al., 2016) play a major role in health outcomes and can become extremely costly. Musich et al. (2018) reported a strong association between health literacy and what they called 'purpose in life', which, in turn, was associated with lower health care utilisation and expenditure, increased compliance with preventive services and higher quality of life. They suggested that higher levels of 'purpose in life' leads to 'successful ageing'.

Moreover, there is a growing body of evidence that self-management interventions for individuals with chronic conditions such as type 2 diabetes can be effective and cost-effective from a societal perspective (Micklethwaite et al.,

2012). For instance, the intervention designed and evaluated by Micklethwaite et al. (2012) saved the respective hospital money primarily by reducing hospital visits. Thus, the hospital could recuperate its total direct annual personnel and operating costs for the initiative, though it had a relatively small number of participants.

Bitzer and Sørensen (2018) found that health literacy appears more and more on public health agendas because it is regarded as a central strategy to reduce health disparities and to design sustainable health care systems. Furthermore, health literacy can be viewed as a way to delegate control towards the general public and patients. This may be viewed as part of the 'new normal of health care'.

3.6 COVID-19: AN EXEMPLARY CASE FOR THE RELEVANCE OF HEALTH LITERACY

A practical example of why health literacy matters was provided by van den Broucke (2020) and Kickbusch (2021), who discuss its role in the context of the COVID-19 pandemic. Van den Broucke (2020) stated that health literacy is a crucial concept in addressing the pandemic, while Kickbusch (2021) suggested four actions for health promotion in response: improve scientific literacy, address the infodemic, address health data extraction and address the political dimensions of health literacy. The COVID-19 pandemic is one of many examples where health information of varying reliability was made available by many different sources and where people were frequently overwhelmed by the amount of data. Readers are referred to van den Broucke (2020) and Kickbusch (2021) for an in-depth analysis.

4

HEALTH LITERACY IN THE 'NEW NORMAL'. . .AND OPPORTUNITIES FOR TECHNOLOGY

4.1 PRESENT SCENARIO

The 'new normal' of health care places patients at its centre where they co-produce their services and co-create value. New technologies aid in expanding the role of digital solutions towards a more integrated, more inclusive system and enable individuals to take a more active part in their health and make informed health care decisions (Conard, 2019). These technologies will be another focal point in this volume.

The role of patients and the general public has changed within the current scenario of the 'new normal' of health care (Marciano et al., 2019). While the 'new normal' explicitly seeks to place patients at the centre of their own health care and have them actively participate, co-produce and co-create, this has become a plain fact of our circumstances. Due to an ever more complex and fragmented health care system, an increasing number of media outlets offering health information (of varying quality and reliability), and a rise in chronic conditions for which patients need to coordinate their care, individuals need to learn how to manage their own care (Hersh et al., 2015). Although the 'new normal' of health care and the patient engagement and involvement that accompany it are viewed as vital aspects of sustainable health systems, scholars find that some determinants of active patient engagement are still widely neglected by both policymakers and health care professionals. Among these neglected factors, inadequate health literacy proves to be a substantial barrier to patient empowerment (Dirmaier & Härter, 2011; Palumbo et al., 2016). About half of subjects in many study samples have been noted to have low health literacy (Palumbo et al., 2016). Section 4.1 takes a closer look at where the issues arise and how new technologies may solve some.

4.1.1 Where to Obtain Health Information and Services

Communication channels differ by target audience. Communication of health information needs to take into account not only the channel but also the target audience's level of health literacy, language preferences and acculturation. For instance, older individuals may prefer conventional channels such as printed media rather than digital media for obtaining their health information (Hillyer et al., 2017). In their study conducted in northern Manhattan, Hillyer et al. (2017) observed that channel preferences varied by age, level of health literacy and education and that adequate health literacy correlated with seeking health information from health care professionals and the internet.

For policymakers, however, it might be more interesting to reach people with low health literacy levels and select the media they are likely to prefer. Zanchetta and Poureslami (2006) studied newcomers to Canada who tend to be unfamiliar with local health care systems. They found that health professionals reported difficulty in communicating with these groups efficaciously, educational resources and approaches only partially reached minorities, and eHealth did not prove effective for users with language and literacy limitations and barriers to accessing information via written material in particular. Consequently, many ethno-cultural groups did not participate in health promotion initiatives.

Problems of adapting to a new health culture stem from a lack of information about the health care available, the subsequent experience with the health care system, and the structural barrier to preventive health care services and formal and informal support networks. Furthermore, the social isolation of newcomers is worsened by linguistic, religious and cultural differences (Zanchetta & Poureslami, 2006). One approach to be kept in mind, regardless of whom one seeks to reach, is to meet people face-to-face in everyday life settings (WHO, 2013): the places where they live, work and play are best suited for transmitting information and where access can be safeguarded and the information trusted.

4.1.1.1 Caregivers and Cultural Settings

Besides for oneself, a person's health literacy will also be relevant for family and friends. Children especially depend for their well-being on their caregiver's health literacy level. Children of parents with high health literacy are more likely to have better outcomes in child health promotion and disease prevention (Sanders et al., 2009). So it makes sense to start health education and teach health literacy early, as it will benefit health later in life (see Section 5.1.2). However, the impact that caregivers and the social environment have should not be neglected either. Bramsved et al. (2018) underlined the importance of health literacy initiatives for the parents of young children. While Hanson et al. (2012) concurred about the decisive role parents play but argued that in low- and middle-income countries, the most promising timing strategy to improve parents' lifestyle, prevent the development of non-communicable diseases like diabetes, and promote health literacy is during adolescence – before pregnancy. They reported that pre-conception interventions are needed to educate prospective parents about making healthy lifestyle choices for themselves and their children. Nevertheless, such health promotion activities require a broader social perspective and a range of multi-sectoral agencies to collaborate. Renzaho et al. (2018) stressed that, among migrant communities in Australia, cultural influences could impact healthy lifestyle choices and that participation in children's health prevention initiatives could be hindered by cultural, family-level and community-level factors.

4.1.1.2 Digital Sources

Information sources of varying degrees of difficulty and detail address different health literacy needs but also pose the problem of varying levels of quality and evidence-based research to back up those claims. Crosswell (2020) asked industry experts about millennial media and found ways in which the media could or could not foster improvement in patient, community and population health outcomes. Among the technologies that have drastically changed how and where we consume information are mobile phones. These devices are destined to play a major role in mobile health (mHealth) and eHealth. They may also help to connect with typically hard-to-reach populations like young people, to collect data and to conduct interventions (Swahn et al., 2014).

In their study, Maggio et al. (2020) examined the online encyclopaedia Wikipedia and sought to train health professional students to critically assess, edit and improve Wikipedia's entries on medical subjects based on evidence-based medicine (EBM). Since Wikipedia is a popular site for seeking medical information, such initiatives may help students and the general public learn about EBM and communication skills.

4.1.1.3 Health Care Organisations

Information acquired directly from a health care organisation will also contribute to the success of an interaction. Palumbo (2021, p. 115) defined organisational health literacy as: 'Organisational health literacy involves the health care organisations' ability to establish an empowering and co-creating relationship with patients, engaging them in the design and delivery of health services in collaboration with health professionals'. Organisational health literacy contributes to the shift towards a patient-centred approach to care and functions complementary to individual health literacy (Palumbo, 2021). One could argue that taking universal health literacy precautions (see Section 7.2) to include people regardless of their level of health literacy is a crucial aspect of organisational health literacy. When health care professionals communicate with patients, the relationship and interaction of organisational health literacy and a patient's health literacy intertwine with one another, which is why organisational health literacy contributes substantially to the outcomes of an interaction.

4.1.1.4 Mass Media

Acquiring information from health care organisations is relevant not only for understanding the information but also for subsequent decision-making. Semakula et al. (2020, 2017) designed an intervention to increase people's ability to critically assess the trustworthiness of claims about the benefits and harms of treatments via a health care podcast. They found that their intervention brought initial improvement in the ability to appraise claims about treatments; however, the skills were drastically decreased one year later. They suggested that such decay could be reduced with more active practice. In their study, Cusack et al. (2018) evaluated initiatives that aim to increase knowledge of comparing claims critically. They reported that studies should be improved in quality and measurement of longer-term effects. In general, the mass media could be a suitable channel to reach people since it is 'where they already are' (WHO, 2013). For practical implications of this strategy, see Section 7.1.5.

4.1.1.5 Health Care Journalists

Shah et al. (2019) reported that health journalists in Pakistan should be trained in local languages at appropriate health literacy levels and cultural sensitivity so they could work as potential partners in national health initiatives. They suggested that the journalists be directly involved in community mobilisation efforts. Health literacy is crucial when numerous stakeholders are involved and how health literate they are and what level of health literacy they adopt when communicating.

4.1.1.6 Health Fairs

Yang et al. (2021) found that attendees of health fairs for Asian and Pacific Islander Americans organised between 2011 and 2018 by a UCLA student-led organisation reported having visited a physician, made lifestyle changes and obtained health insurance since having visited one or more fairs. They suggested that fair attendance remained consistent (despite the health improvements, which would render health fairs less necessary) due to the preference of Asian-American immigrants for health services that are convenient and linguistically and culturally accessible. Such factors should be taken into account when motivating communities to seek care and other health services.

4.1.2 How Information Is Communicated

One needs to take into account an interlocutor's level of health literacy besides social and cultural circumstances. Research shows that health literacy interventions should be adapted to participants' cultural background, especially when dealing with minorities or the disadvantaged (Chiarelli & Edwards, 2006; Dubbin et al., 2021; Ekblad, 2020; Renzaho et al., 2018).

Crosswell (2020) categorised multiple themes of how health care professionals can maintain relevance, access and attainability in their communication: information access, information literacy, patient privacy, patient accountability, physician engagement and health care quality. Levin-Zamir et al. (2021) examined how the COVID-19 pandemic has revealed mismatches between health promotion and national/ global health emergency policies. During a medical crisis, clear communication becomes indispensable; interventions may range from a focus on individuals or families to organisations, communities, health care, public health, education and media systems, health-promoting settings, to policy as a whole. They went on to stress that equity, trust, systems approaches and sustained action in future health promotion preparedness strategies are essential and that clear communication based on health literacy needs to be considered (Levin-Zamir et al., 2021).

In their study, Vargas et al. (2014) examined how plastic surgeons assessed their patients' literacy: 94% of surgeons stated that they use lay terminology, ca. 85% used pictures or diagrams and only about 8% reported using the teach-back method. In this evidence-based communication technique, the interlocutor is solicited to explain back what they were told to assess whether and what they understood correctly (see Section 7.2.2). In general, plastic surgeons overestimated both the level of education and the reading level of their patients compared to national data. Bowskill and Garner (2012) reported that health professionals perform poorly at assessing and identifying patients at risk of low health literacy because they fail to acknowledge the extent of the problem. They suggested that practitioners speak slowly, repeat information, use plain, non-medical language and adopt teach-back methods, as they are easy to adopt and worth the extra time they may take.

Health literacy is also relevant for obtaining consent to treatment or participation in medical research trials since people must understand what they are consenting to. Koonrungsesomboon et al. (2019) tested the applicability and the effectiveness of the enhanced informed consent form methodology in paediatric research, which requires parental consent. They found the enhanced informed consent form to be superior to the conventional one in increasing parental comprehension of trial information. In their study, Ferdinand et al. (2017) examined how labelling and education impact on treatment adherence. They distinguished four areas where additional collaborative research could help to increase comprehension and subsequently reduce non-adherence, two of which are developing patient/ health provider team-based engagement strategies and alleviating health disparities, which intersect with health literacy. Khoong et al. (2018) examined labelling and described an initiative in patient-centred medication labelling. Poor understanding of medication labels and package inserts lead to non-adherence, resulting in reduced health outcomes and patient safety. Patient-centred labelling could contribute to alleviating these potential risks. The initiative is discussed in Section 7.2.3.

4.2 HOW INNOVATION CAN HELP

Communication and understanding of health information are vital factors in health care, health promotion and prevention. Initiatives to overcome obstacles and improve health literacy have been designed for different settings and channels. This section focusses on technological innovations. Innovation and technology have the potential to offer an answer to 'where information is obtained' by design, whether located on a digital platform, a wearable device or a smartphone application. In addition, many technologies also assist in 'how information is communicated'. AI technologies, for example, can adapt their language to the user's health literacy level, cultural background, age or sex. Consideration should be given to new media platforms and their impact on information distribution, adaptive communication strategies when the level of health literacy varies across a population and overall health communication processes. Crosswell (2020) stresses the importance of these factors when discussing the digital shift in health care messaging and its effect on health care outcomes and patient compliance.

To evaluate how innovation and technology can alleviate the problems mentioned in Section 4.1, it is helpful to return to the definition of health literacy. The present volume applies one of the latest all-encompassing definitions also used by the WHO, namely: 'Health literacy is linked to literacy and entails people's knowledge, motivation and competences to access, understand, appraise and apply health information in order to make judgements and take decisions in everyday life concerning health care, disease prevention and health promotion to maintain or improve quality of life during the life course' (Sørensen et al., 2012, p. 83). Fig. 2 presents a graphic illustration translated and adapted from Bitzer and Sørensen (2018). Innovation and technologies may

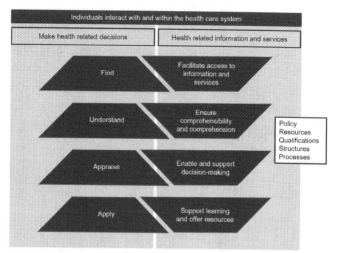

Source: Adapted from Bitzer and Sørensen (2018). Translated by: (Federico Lega and Pia Kreutzer).

Fig. 2. Health Literacy. Individuals Interact With and Within a Health Care System.

facilitate all four steps mentioned above. Examples are given in the following sections.

4.2.1 Find

Bitzer and Sørensen (2018) stated that health-related information and services within a health care system should 'facilitate access to information and services'. The ways in which innovation or technology may do so are manifold: there are apps and platforms where validated health information can be accessed easily without the user having to worry about the quality of the information. Other examples are symptom checkers, where users enter their current symptoms and obtain triage information (e.g. how urgent is the issue? Should one see a doctor or need a referral or emergency services?) or information about differential diagnosis. Differently, wearables display parameters of daily activity (e.g. fitness trackers) or blood glucose levels and blood oxygen levels. Users might not be aware that their current behaviour or habits are suboptimal. There are many more examples of innovative devices that could convey such information and make it immediately accessible.

4.2.2 Understand

To help people understand what they see and hear, 'ensuring comprehensibility and comprehension' is required of health care systems (Bitzer & Sørensen, 2018). Many AI-based innovations target the information specifically to the user's needs and adapt communication and information accordingly (Crosswell, 2020). Understanding may be further facilitated by the fact that one can view it at any given moment, whenever most convenient for the user. In doctor–patient interactions, for example, there typically occur time and resource constraints, as well as constraints on the amount of information that can be absorbed at a time. In general, technologies applied to health literacy could help reduce information asymmetries between health care providers and patients; hence, health innovations could prove to be valuable assets.

4.2.3 Appraise

'Enabling and supporting decision-making' facilitates appraisal, according to Bitzer and Sørensen (2018). Again, there are numerous possibilities for how technology can be helpful. For example, more data about a user's behaviour would be useful in decision-making by a patient's health care team. Deciding between conservative and surgical intervention may be influenced by how active a patient is and whether the surgical intervention is necessary for maintaining the accustomed lifestyle. Such information can be collected by wearables, apps, fitness trackers and the like. For instance, if an activity tracker signals that a user is not as physically active as they should be, a nudge in the right direction may be helpful. Similarly, digital nutrition logs could help users make healthier choices. Symptom checkers may relieve worry about the severity or urgency of an incident or help decide what to do next.

4.2.4 Apply

Applying the information can be aided by 'supporting learning and offering resources', according to Bitzer and Sørensen (2018). Many apps and platforms now provide entertaining ways to learn and implement those learnings. For example, users can be awarded badges for healthy behaviour or be reminded to engage in physical activity or switch to a healthier diet. There are also similar gamified versions that remind users to stop smoking, lose weight, limit alcohol consumption or take their prescription medications. Furthermore, special applications and platforms exist for log entries during pregnancy, during an infant's or toddler's development or to keep track of blood pressure. Increasingly, there are also applications and technologies that support mental health, such as meditation, awareness or general wellness apps. For chronic conditions, virtual nurse systems, for example, can check whether patients have taken their medication, encourage adopting healthy habits and monitor vital signs and symptoms. Similarly, there are 'social companions' for hospitalised patients (Gómez-González et al., 2020) and digital health coaches for various conditions (Lin et al., 2019).

4.3 PROS AND CONS OF TECHNOLOGY

As it is difficult to discuss the benefits of software and hardware as wide-ranging as innovation or technology, the following overview presents the advantages and disadvantages of the currently most popular innovations and applications that impact on health literacy and others examined during the systematic literature review.

The benefits of high health literacy have been discussed in Section 3.1, and how innovation and technology can enhance health literacy. A brief overview of the benefits of innovation and technology is given below.

One of the major advantages of AI is that it can target an individual personally, predict the individual's behaviour and adapt in interaction with the individual (Crosswell, 2020). This feature is particularly convenient in the context of health literacy, since adaption of an individual's level of health literacy is indispensable for understanding and implementation. It is also a prerequisite for patient-centredness. This advantage stems from the adaptability of AI to continuously learn and self-improve with new scientific findings, thus being potentially more up to date than health care professionals themselves (Dilsizian & Siegel, 2014).

Another factor that could support population health management is technology accessibility and availability. Unlike a health care professional, a platform or an application is accessible round the clock and in real time from anywhere in the world, with a low threshold of requirements to be contacted (Dilsizian & Siegel, 2014). This is one of the arguments why technology could help reduce health disparities and inequalities. Nonetheless, there are concerns that insurance companies can access the health data collected by wearables, also when health care systems prevent inequitable medical data mining. Also, there are ethical concerns about bias creation when an AI is trained with inadequate data (Gómez-González et al., 2020; Morley et al., 2020). Either way, data privacy and data security issues remain (Dilsizian & Siegel, 2014), especially in the user's perception of data breaches and generalised lack of trust.

As mentioned in Section 2.1, diagnostic errors are surprisingly common and new technologies could help reduce them, especially those due to cognitive factors and biases (Dilsizian & Siegel, 2014). Also, errors due to human factors (e.g. a health care provider's emotional or physical status) may be avoided. If designed well, technologies have the potential to be more objective. How to benchmark digital health technologies and regulate them (quickly because of the rapid pace of change) remain unresolved issues (Gómez-González et al., 2020).

5

HOW TO IMPROVE HEALTH LITERACY

There are three different approaches to improve health literacy, according to Chiarelli and Edwards (2006): the health system, the education system and the broader sphere of culture and society. The last emphasises that initiatives should be culture-sensitive in design, as mentioned in Section 3.1, where demographic and socio-economic disparities and associations were discussed. Falling within the broader sphere of culture and society are community-organised and community-led interventions. Such an approach interacts with culturally sensitive interventions. There is evidence that local populations, also those that access statutory health services relatively less, may be engaged through such approaches (Brown et al., 2020). Examples of interventions described in the literature review are given below.

5.1 GENERAL INITIATIVES

We have categorised the following initiatives by their approach (health care, education, culture and society). A brief overview of studies on disadvantaged groups will also be given, as this is a central theme in health literacy research.

The initiatives mentioned here are relevant to the 'new normal' of health care as they actively empower patients and help them to co-produce their health care and co-create value. Patient-centredness and population health management are common themes.

5.1.1 Focus on Disadvantaged Groups

Vulnerable groups are frequently the focus of health literacy research because of their greater need. Several recent studies involving disadvantaged groups include Thomas et al. (2019) who interviewed previously incarcerated women who faced challenges of substance abuse, and physical and mental health disorders upon re-entry. King et al. (2019) tested an initiative among African-American women at risk for adverse birth outcomes. Farokhi et al. (2018) conducted a pre-post assessment of an educational intervention on oral health literacy for refugees and other groups. Slewa-Younan et al. (2020) also worked with refugees and their mental health issues. Thomas et al. (2019) reported that the intervention made the women feel supported, motivated and competent to address their health issues. King et al. (2019) stated that their results support the use of preconception health education training and that multi-disciplinary collaboration and targeted interventions may be beneficial when trying to improve the health literacy of minorities. Farokhi et al. (2018) found that all groups, including the refugees, showed considerable improvement in oral health literacy and knowledge of preventive care. Slewa-Younan et al. (2020) found a sustained, noticeable decrease in the refugees' general psychological distress levels and concluded that culturally tailored programmes are essential.

5.1.2 Focus on Teaching and Education

Educational or teaching interventions may take place in all three settings where health literacy initiatives are leveraged. Ammentorp et al. (2021) reviewed studies to determine the main facilitators of and barriers to the implementation of large-scale communication training initiatives based on the Calgary-Cambridge Guide. They evaluated programmes in Australia, Ireland, Austria and Denmark based on RE-AIM factors: Reach, Effectiveness, Adoption, Implementation and Maintenance. The programmes reached their intended target groups. The intervention has been investigated in only two countries so far, but new courses are planned. The main challenge was that the implementation, including educating the trainers, rested on just a few persons. The authors stated that large-scale communication training initiatives can be carried out in multiple health care settings, while it is vital to standardise trainer education and then adapt the programmes to clinical practice. Also, to ensure sustainability and address the potential for scale up, resources need to be prioritised and allocated at the political and organisational level (Ammentorp et al., 2021).

Micklethwaite et al. (2012) designed and evaluated a self-management intervention for individuals with type 2 diabetes in a community general hospital targeting under-served people with barriers to obtaining regular health care. The initiative focussed on improving access to care, increasing health literacy and collaborating with the individuals to make long-term lifestyle changes.

Leger (2001) identified the interface between a school's core objective of education and public health goals. He argued that there is a notable overlap between the success of a health-promoting school and an effective school. Examples in nutrition convey how the link between education and health literacy commitments can operate in schools. For more information on health-promoting schools, see Section 7.1.6.

5.1.3 Focus on Patient Support Groups

Wu et al. (2020) studied patient support groups (PSGs) and how to improve their quality. They focussed on PSGs in a hospital but a PSG can also be community-based or conducted in an educational setting. The quality of the PSGs was enhanced over the course of three years through the use of standardised protocols to apply for financial support and reporting results, and initiatives that honour and improve peer support and health literacy initiatives based on questionnaire responses. Over the three years, participation by patients, their families and staff increased, and more interdisciplinary curricula were generated. Wu et al. (2020) identified the enlisting of a core change team, the creation of a stakeholder map and the selection of an improvement framework as the factors that led to good results.

5.1.4 Focus on Health Systems

Community pharmacies in Australia and New Zealand deliver health information through Self Care Cards that cover diverse health topics (e.g. signs and symptoms, when to see a doctor, etc.). Coughlan et al. (2012) evaluated whether such an initiative could also be applied in Ireland and examined the relevance of health literacy in this context. While about 89% of participants reported liking the concept and 83% stated that the cards helped them understand their health issues, the pilot cards were at too high a health literacy level for the general Irish public. These results show that it makes sense for interventions – while appreciated by patients and distributed as practical methods to communicate health information – to be checked for the health literacy level of the target audience and whether it is adequate for its intended purposes.

5.1.5 Focus on Society and Culture: The Case for Health Fairs

Theoretically, health fairs could be part of all three approaches; the example fits into the society and culture category. As mentioned in Section 4.1.1, Yang et al. (2021) examined health fairs held from 2011 to 2018 by a UCLA student-led organisation for Asian and Pacific Islander Americans. The fair attendees reported having visited a physician, made lifestyle changes and purchased health insurance after visiting one or more fairs. Fair attendance remained consistent (although the improved health behaviours might have rendered the health fairs superfluous) because Asian-American immigrants prefer health services that are convenient as well as linguistically and culturally accessible. Such factors should be taken into account when motivating communities to seek medical care and other health services.

5.1.6 Focus on Health Professional Capacity Building

Many initiatives also focussed on programmes specifically designed for health care professionals to help raise awareness, educate or train them in health literacy or increase organisational health literacy. This section gives a brief overview of several initiatives.

The Agency for Healthcare Research and Quality Health Literacy Universal Precautions Toolkit was designed to assist primary care practitioners in evaluating and improving communication with their patients. According to the qualitative study conducted by Mabachi et al. (2016), the practitioners recommended reducing the toolkit's information density and making specific refinements. A similar intervention was designed by Koops van't Jagt et al. (2016); the intervention showed promising results to improve the communicative health literacy of older individuals but needed further evaluation.

Galiatsatos et al. (2015) evaluated the Lay Health Educator Programme, in which resident physicians were trained to advance their understanding of health literacy and the health concerns of laypersons. There was a statistically significant change in the physicians' comprehension of what the public views as important about specific health care topics. However, the study sample size was relatively small, with only 15 participants.

As mentioned in Section 4.1.1, Maggio et al. (2020) sought to provide medical professional students with the necessary skillset to critically assess, edit and improve medical content in the online encyclopaedia Wikipedia by applying the concepts of evidence-based medicine (EBM). Such an initiative might not only be helpful for the students to grasp the principles of EBM but also to improve their communication skills and Wikipedia's health topics entries, which are oftentimes among the first internet sites where users seek health information. According to Maggio et al. (2020), future areas of this initiative will include guidelines for students on how to write in simple language and communicate with written material.

Harper et al. (2007) described approaches to improve medical students' awareness of health literacy, ability to communicate clearly, and strategies to ensure patient understanding and successfully communicate with individuals with limited health literacy.

5.2 TECHNOLOGIES THAT COULD CHANGE HOW PEOPLE ARE EDUCATED AND EMPOWERED

An overview of the advantages and the potential drawbacks of technological innovation was given in Section 4.3. This section presents practical examples of the technologies.

To be able to make use of one's health literacy and derive desirable health outcomes from it, one also needs to be able to access and use health and health care services, interact with a health care professional and carry out self-care. Digital services may support these actions, insofar as they are designed to simplify or expand on a specific health topic or concept or to test one's comprehension, without time or location constraints. Scholars agree that new technologies like AI, machine learning, virtual and augmented reality, and blockchain can shift technology beyond mere data collection towards a more integrated system. Digital solutions can enable people to participate in their health and decision-making proactively. They enable multimedia education that can combine video, voice and print at graded health literacy levels in diverse languages by applying formal and informal teaching methods (Conard, 2019).

One example is massive open online courses (MOOCs), which are increasingly offered in health care and medicine on various platforms. When available from reputable institutions, they can provide a reliable source of information without time, location or educational constraints. MOOCs can increase the public's health literacy, provide access to evidence-based information and education, and explore innovative teaching methods when designed and developed collaboratively. They could thus facilitate effective communication between patients and health care professionals, while collecting data through large-scale measurement and analysis. These data, in turn, could augment the understanding of disease risk and of health prevention, and so improve medical education and patient-centred techniques for student learning (Goldberg & Crocombe, 2017).

Rezaei Aghdam et al. (2020) focussed on patient-driven service innovations, digital health platforms and online health communities (OHCs). They claimed that while such innovations can increase patient participation and constitute a potential for health care organisations, they also pose challenges. Nonetheless, the salient themes were: communication extension, improved health literacy for patients and health care organisations, transparent communication with patients, informational and social support for patients, and patient empowerment in self-management. The study also reported that OHCs can be used to derive new knowledge from data generated by patient interactions, which could then be applied to support health care organisations in customising treatment plans and communicating effectively and transparently with their patients. Some studies, however, contested the use of OHCs to provide accurate informational and emotional support or empower patients in their self-management (Rezaei Aghdam et al., 2020).

The role of innovative technologies and mobile phones with regard to non-communicable diseases (NCDs) was investigated by Tabassum et al. (2018). The study setting was Bangladesh, where health literacy is low and people are less receptive to health information and less likely to adopt healthy behaviours.

One approach to reach people is via mass media, which can play a crucial role in promoting healthy habits. Examples from different countries concern the use of mass media campaigns for NCDs and prevention initiatives. Mass media as a communication channel have been discussed (see Section 4.1.1 and implications for policymakers will later be discussed in Section 7.1.5).

To decrease rural health disparities, the University of Wisconsin Carbone Cancer Center launched an evidence-based education programme that can be locally adapted for use in rural Wisconsin communities. Through multi-step community involvement efforts, the programme was also culturally tailored to African-American and Latino populations. It comprises modules on cancer basics, prevention and screening; all adaptations are built upon health literacy principles and aimed to improve health-related decision-making. Current efforts are underway to gather more evidence for the programme's effectiveness, expand its use and adapt it into a web-based platform that features a cancer prevention game (Fredrick et al., 2020).

Brian and Ben-Zeev (2014) examined the possibilities of mHealth in Asia for the study, diagnosis and treatment of mental health disorders. They described how mHealth programmes could increase mental health literacy, enhance access to mental health services, expand community-based outreach and engagement, bolster capabilities to self-manage illness and regulate medication distribution. They also reported potential barriers and limitations of mHealth for mental health, such as funding, language and literacy, power supply, data security and privacy issues.

OpenNotes, an initial research initiative exploring how to share medical notes with patients to improve their understanding of health care, is tackling the problem of clinicians' limited time to explain health concepts or deliver health information to their patients. Giving patients access to their medical notes has been shown to have advantages, including improved patient satisfaction and clinical outcomes. Nevertheless, clinicians have voiced concern that OpenNotes may require them to spend time to explain in clear terms the medical language in the notes.

One of the many health-related applications of AI technology is conversion of medical to plain language, which shortens clinicians' time with their patients. Bala et al. (2020) tested the AI translated version of medical notes versus standard medical language; however, the statistical analysis was underpowered to determine a significant difference. Findings from the guided interviews with patients suggested that simplified plain-language notes may be more useable, improve the patient–clinician relationship and empower patients through improved understanding of their health care (Bala et al., 2020). Further research is needed to assess the effectiveness and cost-effectiveness of similar tools.

eHealth tools are innovative ways to address the health literacy of university students reporting limited access to health care services, high rates of avoidance/delay in seeking medical care and trouble obtaining health-related information. Montagni et al. (2017) co-created a web-app that mapped and described free or low-cost health services available in Bordeaux, France, specifically for university students. The development of such apps could benefit from stakeholder involvement of students as prospective users and health care providers to correctly identify and display relevant health care services.

Patient portals are another channel for patients to obtain health information about chronic conditions. Older patients seem reluctant to access patient portals as they prefer traditional information channels (see Section 4.1.1). There has been a lack of support to improve this in many implementation processes. Nahm et al. (2019) assessed the impact of an older adult-friendly theory-based patient portal e-Learning programme on patient portal knowledge, selected health outcomes (e.g. decision-making self-efficacy and health communication), patient portal self-efficacy and use, and eHealth literacy of older individuals. Three weeks after the initiative, greater improvement in all variables except patient portal use was noted for the intervention group; however, the improvement disappeared within four months. While the findings show that the programme improved selected health and patient portal use outcomes, more research on long-term effects needs to be conducted with more diverse samples (Nahm et al., 2019). Again, cost-effectiveness should be closely examined.

Users of the US health care system are increasingly engaged in digital health technologies when they want to enrol in care, gain access to personal health information, interact with health care providers or monitor their health. However, to do so may be more difficult for disadvantaged populations with low health literacy, time restraints or competing priorities. Guendelman et al. (2017) wanted to assess the adoption and use of digital health tools among disadvantaged first-time pregnant women and mothers of young children: 97% of participants stated they had searched for health information on the internet during the past year, 42% did not engage in digital health-management. Among low- and non-users, 49% expressed interest in using digital health tools in the future. Study sample demographics were not found to be major drivers of digital health use. The study reported that disparities in digital health tool use should be addressed, otherwise the benefits of digital tools will accrue predominantly to individuals with the resources and the ability to use them anyway.

Gbadamosi et al. (2018) examined the role of electronic health platforms and noted that since most depend on the availability of internet connectivity, their use is limited in many rural or resource-limited settings. In response, they developed an integrated mHealth platform to collect medical information such as test results and encrypt them on a patient-held smartcard. The information can be decrypted at the point of care without an internet connection. Projects focussing on digital app implementation in resource-limited settings or for disadvantaged populations will be crucial to diminish health disparities.

Taylor et al. (2020) found that mHealth strategies have the unequalled potential to prevent chronic disease (e.g. cardio-vascular disease) or improve self-management among African-Americans and other ethnic minorities. With the MOYO app and its cloud-based data collection infrastructure, changes in health variables, including passive (e.g. activity levels and sleep parameters), active (e.g. mood measures and surveys) measures, and external factors (e.g. weather and socio-economic indicators), were collected and used to train machine-learning algorithms and then to regress them on self-reported quality of life variables. The project will provide valuable information about community co-creation of mHealth initiatives, add to the knowledge of exposure and behaviour that impact health, and act as a channel for inter-ventions, clinical trials and improvement in health literacy (Taylor et al., 2020).

Benis et al. (2021) explored the concept of One Digital Health, wherein One Health and digital health are combined. One Digital Health is constructed around three perspectives (individual health and well-being; population and society; ecosystem) and five dimensions (citizen engagement, educa-tion, environment, human and veterinary health care, health care industry 4.0). According to Benis et al. (2021, p. 1) 'One Digital Health aims to digitally transform future health eco-systems, by implementing a systemic health and life sciences approach that takes into account broad digital technology perspectives on human health, animal health, and the man-agement of the surrounding environment'. In this hybrid landscape, individuals and their health data are central to the acquisition and the management of individual-level and population-level data. For the interaction between One Digital Health and digital health communities to be effective, near real-time data and data-driven input in systems medicine and systems ecology are necessary. Health literacy, digital health literacy, and collaboration in the prevention, control and solution of potential problems are further prerequisites (Benis et al., 2021).

Mwaisaka et al. (2021) assessed digital health usability in their study investigating on-demand mHealth platforms for sexual and reproductive health. They reported that taking a wide range of health literacy levels and technological variants into account cannot be stressed enough when dealing with young people.

Costa et al. (2021) targeted sexual and sexual and reproductive health behaviour among young people. They presented a community-based social prescribing and digital intervention in Cape Verde, which will be developed over 3 years. In the meantime, Costa et al. (2021) claimed that it will contribute to sexual and reproductive health-related health literacy and quality of life across the life course of young people.

Technological innovation has also proven useful in the context of the COVID-19 pandemic. Intawong et al. (2021) examined the creation and the implementation of application technologies to support the battle against COVID-19. They studied a technology that assisted patients and potential patients in evaluating their symptoms and installed a rapid tracking mechanism until public health surveillance was established. Another example is a patient and hospital management system supporting the monitoring of COVID-19 patients via an interconnected network of hospitals. Intawong et al. (2021) stated that the application proved effective in promoting health, improving patient satisfaction, curtailing readmission rates and extending health resources.

Summarising, these technologies and digital interventions afford some of the most pertinent advantages of innovation. Although their long-term impact has not yet been studied, they have the potential to reduce health disparities and delegate decisions to patients and the general public. Such trends align with patient-centredness, population health management and the 'new normal' of health care, which makes them highly relevant for the intersection of health literacy, technological innovation, and the 'new normal'. They thus need further development and evaluation.

5.3 WHAT WE SHOULD KNOW ABOUT EHEALTH LITERACY

There remain ample research gaps in the effectiveness and cost-effectiveness of health literacy initiatives. One area where there is much need for further study is eHealth programmes that overlap with health literacy objectives. Eng (2001, p. 267) defines eHealth as 'the use of emerging information and communication technology, especially the Internet, to improve or enable health and health care'. When combining the concepts of health literacy and eHealth, one seeks to examine the knowledge, motivation and competences to access, understand, appraise and apply health information from information and communication technology, especially the internet, to make judgements and take decisions in everyday life concerning health care, disease prevention and health promotion to maintain or improve quality of life.

Norman and Skinner (2006b) used a similar combination of these two concepts, albeit with different definitions. With increasing popularity of the internet as a source for health information, eHealth literacy has also gained importance. The publicly available data on private eHealth services (e.g. applications, fitness trackers, wearables, eHealth literacy itself) are incredibly scarce. This has implications not only for the scientific community but also for policymakers, health care managers, consumers, patients and communities. Within 'the new normal' of health care, eHealth literacy has become critical because it may offer a way to reduce health literacy disparities, to 'meet people where they already are' and reach them, and to render health care more patient-centred when implemented carefully and culturally sensitive. With the coinciding rise of patient-centredness, co-creation and co-production, and digital means and technological innovation having a profound impact on society and health, eHealth literacy has become the link between these two concepts and how they interact.

The associations and relevance of health literacy have been discussed in Section 3.1; however, little information or evidence is available about eHealth literacy, a future area of research.

6

CLINICAL PATHWAYS AS A MANAGEMENT TOOL TO ENHANCE HEALTH LITERACY[1]

The World Health Organization (WHO) defines health literacy as the reasoned propensity of individuals to improve the community and their health by changing lifestyle and living conditions. The literature identifies health literacy as one of the main determinants of good health outcomes, yet the WHO also reports that many countries find it difficult to raise their literacy rates to a basic level, such as the ability to identify risk factors and understand their effects (Nutbeam, 2020). Nonetheless, in their effort to reduce the demand for health services, government policies urge patients and healthy citizens to visit prevention services and to limit their exposure to risk factors.

The scientific literature reports on the impact health literacy has on patient health outcomes and primary and secondary prevention; accordingly, health service decision-makers marshal their efforts to borrow good practices for increasing the literacy rate of health service users. In the rationalisation of resources and the reorganisation of service delivery models consequent to the 'unkind push' by the COVID-19 pandemic, social and health care workers have had to align professionally.

---

1 This chapter was written by Elena Maggioni, University of Milan.

Also, health care systems require more from the community. Placing these needs in parallel with new trajectories in the provision of services (telemedicine, digital therapeutics, precision medicine and patient-centred hospitals), the community seems to be the appropriate setting for defining and implementing awareness strategies targeted to service users. For example, clinical pathways are one tool that health system policymakers can use to improve health literacy effectively.

Appropriately constructed clinical pathways create clearer paths of management and care by standardising and rationalising activities and actors. From a service user's perspective, clinical pathways help navigate a health care system and understand the steps for correctly continuing along a treatment path. Health literacy plays a key role in this. While clinicians and health professionals can easily read and follow the indications for a clinical pathway, often summarised in flow charts, service users often cannot. Paradoxically, health systems are increasingly difficult to navigate even by educated users. Schools may fail to provide users with adequate skills to access, understand and apply health information to improve their health status.

To overcome this cultural and social barrier, patient associations should be involved in defining clinical pathways. This would ensure that user-friendly materials are created that describe activities to improve health literacy. The material design may be transversal to different pathways since the activities address not only patients entering a specific clinical path but all service users. According to the literature, health promotion activities that foster literacy are information and documentation and public training/information meetings for defined target audiences. Activities that can be institutionalised in clinical pathways involve the definition of multi-dimensional information in multi-disciplinary tables by clinicians and the identification of the distributors of such information. This would ensure that the health care system presents as a single entity, despite the numerous actors involved. The engagement of third sector and local agencies in health literacy promotion in schools and community events is a health policy issue.

Moreover, besides institutionalising activities to promote health literacy, verifying a service user's level in encounters with the health care system is fundamental for establishing a relationship with patients. Assessment of a patient's health literacy in clinical practice is generally done by a health care professional. But judging a patient's health literacy level may cause embarrassment (Scovino, 2021). Setting a point within a clinical pathway for evaluating a patient's level of skills and knowledge could make for more appropriate interventions by health staff and better communication between staff and patients. Such assessment could further inform the drafting and implementation of clinical pathways.

The health literacy rate should be included among the variables for stratifying a population's fragility. Health literacy may be considered a predictor of a population's health status (Scovino, 2021), especially for chronic conditions, since health care systems need to be able to evaluate the probability of mismanagement (Howley, 2004). In the preliminary phase of clinical pathway development, health literacy evaluation could be part of planning care pathways for an ageing population and for young people uninformed about unhealthy behaviours such as alcohol and tobacco use.

Clinical pathways can be employed to engage and empower clinical and non-clinical stakeholders in achieving medical and economic objectives. Pathways within the work ecosystem of a health organisation can foster group cohesion among professionals. The scientific literature and the surveys carried out in various different contexts underscore the capacity of such documents. Provision of occasions for reflection and dialogue between professionals during the drafting of clinical pathways can create bridges between professionals and foster a single vision of patient admission and care.

Health literacy comprises the ability to understand a doctor's words and to navigate a health system's pathways. But how can a service user learn to navigate them if the system does not present itself properly? Technically, health literacy does not refer to health care professionals; however, clinicians may fail to transfer health knowledge to their patients. Because of lack of a single vision by health care professionals, patients need to weigh different voices, opinions and recommendations, and frequently do not know which to follow. A deficit in health literacy does not help users who rely for health information on the web more than on health professionals. Clinical pathways, comprising health prevention, that are readily comprehensible and easy to read (user-friendly) can help users enter the dynamics of a health system. To ensure that physicians take a crucial part in fostering literacy, they should be engaged in health prevention and admission pathways. The institutionalisation of occasions for dialogue between professionals and the definition of governance could provide reference points to express opinions and encourage participation in a health care team to which they feel they belong.

Emergency room overcrowding results from mismanagement of cases in the community. Although the involvement of all health and non-health professionals (third sector, social services) is salient to the literacy process, the first points of contact with the health system are fundamental. The reorganisation of the health care system in Italy, for example, is changing how this happens. To start, general practitioners (GPs) are one of the first points of reference for service users, or at least they should be. GPs may recognise patients with low health literacy, quantify the deficits and recommend ad hoc solutions. Low health literacy may be linked to low attention or propensity to self-care or advanced age and lack of family members and caregivers. Mapping these situations is key to stratifying a population. However, engagement by general medicine could be more complex, to the detriment of health professionals working in hospitals. Clinical pathways cannot be tools of engagement if left to themselves. To correctly engage community medicine and GPs, the general directors of health organisations should develop multi-disciplinary and multi-professional team activities in various different care settings. First, the creation of local hospital networks, institutionalised in devoted admission and care pathways. In daily practice, the general directors will have to incorporate formal and informal occasions into their agendas to deal with community and hospital members of multi-disciplinary teams, including the welcome kits that make new GPs and community workers feel part of a health care organisation. The clinical pathways become a tool to institutionalise and ritualise the link between the hospital and the community in building a common strategy to accompany patients along their treatment path. In this way, patients can acquire skills and knowledge in health literacy.

Besides GPs and paediatricians, case managers also can play a central role in fostering the health literacy of patients and caregivers. Case managers cover diverse specialities from the local GP to the family nurse. Health care decision-makers need to train case managers to transmit their knowledge and skills in disease management to patients and caregivers so that they can manage the illness and make lifestyle changes as necessary.

One of the objectives of a health care system is to support healthy citizens in making healthy lifestyle choices and encourage use of prevention and diagnosis services. In daily practice, health care organisations will have to equip community health workers with information material, also in digital format, to reach healthy citizens and caregivers during contact time. By word-of-mouth recommendation, health care agencies can have a major voice in disseminating accurate information to contrast the unreliable information found on the web.

Just as clinical pathways can have an impact on health literacy and engagement by community medicine so too literacy impacts on the application of clinical pathways. Higher health skills of users can raise awareness of risk factors and adherence to prevention, screening and treatment. Studies on the need for health systems to teach their users how to manage their illness have identified flexible strategies, available resources and achievable targets.

Technology plays a central role in this: from telemedicine to digital therapeutics, physicians can monitor their patients remotely, while patients can learn about their illness and how to manage it. The main difficulties with the use of new technologies lie in teaching patients, their caregivers and clinicians how to use them. Furthermore, a health care organisation should have reference points to support users (both patients and professionals). In this regard, it may be preferable for institutions to designate a reference person for innovation management and training and local health departments, whose job is to coordinate the organisation's training of professionals in the use of these technologies so that they can transfer their knowledge to patients.

In conclusion, health literacy is a field for all players in a health care system. Government and health care decision-makers will need to step up their efforts to reach service users and encourage willingness to learn. However, such efforts cannot (and must not) be directed solely to the creation of documents explaining how to use resources more efficiently and increase the cost-effectiveness of the national (or regional) health care system. They will need to be oriented towards assessing the health literacy of users who interface with the health care system and undertaking action to fill knowledge gaps. Furthermore, health care organisations should recommend reliable health care information sources so that users become an equal partner in the doctor–patient relationship. Greater responsibility taken on by community medicine could help health care organisations in reaching users directly through health care professionals to help them make healthy lifestyle choices and correct use of health care services. Due to the vast organisational, managerial and context variables and available resources, it would be impractical to list the activities and the tools that a health care organisation can use. Health care decision-makers will have to plan community interventions and act nationally. Clinical pathways can be used as a tool to standardise these interventions. Furthermore, doctors and specialists will need to be willing (or be persuaded by their organisations) to work with patients and their caregivers in acquiring health knowledge: engagement of professionals is essential for health literacy to become common ground for users, community medicine and the economic-managerial objectives of a health care system.

7

IMPLICATIONS AND LESSONS FOR HEALTH POLICYMAKERS AND HEALTH MANAGERS

This volume has presented evidence for why health literacy matters in health outcomes and health disparities. Numerous health literacy initiatives that intersect with 'the new normal' of health care have been discussed with a focus on technological innovation. The present findings have been reorganised and framed into areas of action for both policymakers and health care organisations, as well as implications and recommendations for Europe. The systematic review of the literature refers to research conducted in Europe and the developed countries. There is ample space for research in the developing countries and the extra-European context.

7.1 FOR POLICYMAKERS

Most actions proposed here match with those identified by the World Health Organization (WHO (2013)). They have been further enriched and framed according to the challenges of the 'new normal' of health care in the last decade. The first five recommendations have broad ranging implications, while the others relate to specific policy areas.

7.1.1 Health and Health Literacy as a Public Good

The WHO stresses that health-related rights and access to information are key and that the population must be able to advance their health, avert (unnecessary) disease and cope with chronic conditions. Health information and navigable health care systems are seen as fundamental rights. As discussed in Section 1.1, health literacy is a public health imperative. However, health literacy typically locates along a social gradient, where low health literacy is linked to suboptimal ability to adequately self-manage health, obtain health care, comprehend relevant information and make informed decisions. Survey results show that 50% of Europeans have inadequate or problematic health literacy scores and that action needs to be taken. It is the responsibility of policymakers to reduce such health inequities. Technological innovation could help to do so, but it might also exacerbate the issue if implemented without community involvement. Initiatives should be targeted and adjusted to the needs of vulnerable populations, whose cultural sensitivity also needs to be taken into account (Slewa-Younan et al., 2020; Yang et al., 2021). Health literacy is a crucial factor not only for individual health outcomes but also bears a cost burden for individuals and their families, health systems and society as a whole. Raising health literacy is a long-term strategic goal that demands long-term investment. Governments and international agencies need to step in to provide supportive environments committed to achieving adequate health literacy as a goal of health policy and education policy, incorporated into outcome measures, school curricula and lifelong learning. Improved health literacy is a sustainable goal that supports people in managing their health (WHO, 2013). As such, it also plays a vital role in health care system sustainability despite rising health care costs.

7.1.2 The Need for Advocacy and Leadership

Many stakeholders should be involved to endorse and implement health literacy initiatives actively. Some countries have established health literacy networks among stakeholders and organisations to advance patient empowerment and health promotion. Corporate social responsibility should provide for accurate and comprehensible information about product and marketing claims. The media and the communications industry should collaborate to ensure the exchange of information. Furthermore, international and regional agencies may be powerful platforms for action. These interactions were vital before the 'new normal' and are gaining importance with increased connectedness and ease of access to information via electronic and digital technologies. Policymakers need to be aware of this interplay so they can lead the way to enhancing health literacy by using these networks to inform well-designed policies. Policymakers should recognise the cruciality of health literacy for public health and see it as an integral part of their agenda. By implementing standards for health-literate organisations, they can steer public and private stakeholders beyond the health care industry towards the adoption of health literacy-friendly actions. Multidimensional approaches will be needed to reach the general public. Such programmes are best integrated into everyday life settings and adapted to cultural diversity, gender and age in design and distribution channel. Many countries have established agencies devoted to improving low health literacy rates (WHO, 2013).

7.1.3 The Need for Data

The current lack of evidence is a vexing issue for health literacy research. More data need to be collected and analysed. First, there is a lack of data on health literacy itself. For all age groups, surveys investigating health literacy and the health literacy-friendliness of health care systems should be conducted at regular intervals. Only with such data will it be possible to evaluate the effectiveness of single initiatives and to develop national and international evaluation frameworks of health literacy and health literacy-friendliness, as well as compare progress in health literacy between countries. While many studies have focussed on the effectiveness of programmes for health literacy improvement, few have evaluated their long-term effectiveness and long-term cost-effectiveness. However, the present measures of health literacy might not suffice for such purposes. As mentioned in Section 2.1, many scholars acknowledge that there is a shift underway from individual health literacy towards a public health perspective on collective levels and communities (WHO, 2013). To improve methods for evaluating health literacy initiatives and policies, the WHO recommends developing a set of indicators that cover a broad range of health literacy domains that are applicable at regional and national levels so that the set can be applied across multiple settings (WHO Health Evidence Network, 2019).

7.1.4 Collaborating to Speed Up Progress

European organisations should collaborate on expanding the European Health Literacy Survey so that it is continuously funded, conducted regularly and in more countries with the support of the European Union, the WHO and the Member

States. Collaborative efforts in data generation and research can serve to assess the effectiveness of policies and benchmark the results of specific groups. 'Zooming in' on vulnerable populations or on regional and national differences is possible only when enough data points are present. Furthermore, European centres of excellence should be supported to maintain the momentum of health literacy, foster a scientific and a policy agenda, and extend health literacy networks. The European Union and health care agencies such as the WHO Regional Office for Europe should cooperate with other international stakeholders in this area of health action, especially for promoting health innovation. Coordination may be particularly fruitful owing to the growing importance of eHealth and the new media in stimulating health literacy and the potential problems of regulating health innovations. Such networks could also facilitate learning networks, like the Health Literacy Europe network, where professionals work in research, policy and practice. Through these strategies designed at the national, regional and local level, everyone can progress faster (WHO, 2013).

7.1.5 Deep-Dive: Policy Action in Media and Communication

Communication of health and risk factors needs to be clear and transparent. Regulations restricting the advertising of tobacco and alcohol products should be enforced and space devoted to health-promotion information. Social media and mass media open unprecedented opportunities for transmitting health messages but can also be used for spreading misinformation. Quality assurance to counteract false information must be required of all information sources, for example, regulation of health claims and criteria of information and accreditation schemes for health literacy-friendly information.

Moreover, policymakers and public agencies may offer reliable and readily understandable, high-quality information themselves or through reputable, independent partner institutions. These steps will aid in helping citizens to distinguish between fact and fiction in health information. Individual and population health literacy may be enhanced by tailoring information via adequate channels that deliver audience-centred health messages encouraging healthy behaviour. Strategies in commercial advertising can also be applied, such as targeting and market segmentation. Educational entertainment (edutainment), interpersonal communication and multimedia approaches have proven effective in many contexts.

Another development is the importance eHealth literacy has gained in the context of 'the new normal'. Electronic health literacy applies the principles of health literacy to health information from electronic sources. Since electronic media and channels are increasingly pervasive in our day-to-day lives and the health sector, eHealth literacy is becoming more and more relevant. There are, however, concerns about equity. Poorly implemented eHealth literacy initiatives could exacerbate the equity issues mentioned in Section 4.1, as only a certain subset of the population has the means to access and understand online electronic health information. However, eHealth literacy would also help reduce these disparities especially when eHealth information is tailored specifically to population sub-groups. Tailored health information designed with accessibility and equity in mind can help diminish health disparities.

In addition, policy interventions and health information are most useful if available where people already go rather than creating new platforms that only a sub-group of the population will find and access. Social media can take a crucial part

(WHO, 2013). Nonetheless, with health innovations playing an increasingly vital role, there is also the need for adequate regulation of medtech devices and platforms. eHealth literacy and its association with health outcomes are discussed in Section 5.3.

7.1.6 Deep-Dive: Policy Action in Education

Health and education are interdependent and need to be addressed as such. Only healthy citizens can fulfil their potential and achieve success and productivity in their work lives. As stated in Section 2.1, education and knowledge about healthy behaviour, risk factors and the health care system are a part of health literacy and crucial determinants of health, which is why educational interventions are essential to promote and improve health literacy. The foundation for health literacy should be laid in early childhood when children are eager to learn and the benefits of learning can last a lifetime. Early childhood education programmes, interaction with family and friends, and innovative concepts such as health-promoting schools can contribute to the essential know-how and skills that help to maintain health and health literacy. Learning does not stop after school graduation, however. Policies should address barriers that create social inequities in education, health and health literacy, such as costs, lack of awareness of options and lack of interest. While each of these issues may need to be addressed differently, a learning programme for improving health literacy skills will benefit course participants as well as their families. A combined approach may be best crafted using multimedia and tailored to a target audience. The latter implies understanding and working with audience perceptions, attitudes, behaviours, learning and media channel preferences. Furthermore, educational techniques that allow for active participation and invite contemplation and open discussion are promising strategies that can engage both adults and children to access, understand, appraise and apply health information (WHO, 2013).

7.1.7 Deep-Dive: Policy Action in the Marketplace and Communities

Policy action can set the conditions of a navigable environment for service users through clear labelling and information (e.g. the number of calories in a food or beverage product), nudging strategies (opting-in vs. opting-out strategies), consumer-right-to-know and product liability laws. Additionally, public agencies can ensure or provide pertinent, coherent and evidence-based health information by either making it mandatory (e.g. labelling of product characteristics) or having reputable public institutions or independent partners provide them. Counselling and advocacy are other instruments public agencies can use to ensure adequate informedness.

Moreover, successful interventions often initiate action where people are already present, where they live, work and spend time, and use multiple approaches, as discussed in Section 7.1. They should accommodate different learning styles and cultural backgrounds and use multiple approaches simultaneously (e.g. awareness raising, industry regulations on the information provided). Nudging techniques may have a positive influence on people's behaviour for choosing healthier options. In line with the 'new normal' of health care, such actions allow people to actively participate, co-create and co-produce (World Health Organization, 2013).

7.2 FOR HEALTH MANAGERS

Health (care) organisations and their managers play a central role in developing health literacy. According to the Institute of Medicine Roundtable on Health Literacy (2012, p. 3) there are 10 attributes of a health-literate health care organisation:

1. 'Has leadership that makes health literacy integral to its mission, structure, and operations'

2. 'Integrates health literacy into planning, evaluation measures, patient safety, and quality improvement'

3. 'Prepares the workforce to be health literate and monitors progress'

4. 'Includes populations served in the design, implementation, and evaluation of health information and services'

5. 'Meets the needs of populations with a range of health literacy skills while avoiding stigmatization'

6. 'Uses health literacy strategies in interpersonal communications and confirms understanding at all points of contact'

7. 'Provides easy access to health information and services and navigation assistance'

8. 'Designs and distributes print, audio-visual, and social media content that is easy to understand and act on'

9. 'Addresses health literacy in high-risk situations, including care transitions and communications about medicines'

10. 'Communicates clearly what health plans cover and what individuals will have to pay for services'

Mabachi et al. (2016) noted that if a health care organisation adopts most of these practices, they will be more receptive to people's demands, particularly people with low health literacy, and contribute to enhancing population health. However, few studies to date have assessed how far organisations are currently adopting these practices. Howe et al. (2020) found that there is limited leadership and little systemic promotion of efforts to ensure that health-literate health care organisations share these attributes. Some organisations have adopted creative programmes and solutions, however. To ensure that attention is being paid to health literacy, health literacy awareness should be a quality criterion for health care management. Applying universal precautions is relevant for both health care professionals and health care organisations. Internal programme evaluation should include health literacy measures, where users must be included in planning, governance, quality assurance and improvement. This would help to create a shame-free environment where individuals feel comfortable about asking questions or soliciting help, where they feel welcomed, and support is offered, where signage, forms and labels are clear and understandable, materials are carefully devised for implementation, and communication is attentive, helpful and written in plain language (WHO, 2013).

7.2.1 Barriers and Facilitators

Mabachi et al. (2016) identified the challenges of primary care practices implementing a toolkit to improve health literacy, such as competing demands, bureaucratic obstacles, technological barriers, little experience in quality improvement and limited leadership support. The importance of a practice champion, who might most effectively be in a leadership position, was reported by Dowrick et al. (2013). They described the complex role of receptionists in negotiating access to initiatives and the engagement facilitated by prior training knowledge and a sense of co-production. Similarly, in an initiative for patient-centred labelling, Khoong et al. (2018) found that pharmacists were reluctant to modify prescriber instructions and that time constraints were barriers. In contrast, leadership, policy directives and communication networks with prescribers were perceived as facilitators. It seems that convincing staff, and leadership especially, of the benefits of such initiatives and 'getting them on board' is indispensable.

While health literacy-friendliness is crucial in everyday life to maintain population health, it will also be vital in health care organisations to improve suboptimal health status by creating health literacy-friendly health care settings. Health professionals should perceive their communication skills and advance their patients' health literacy as a means to enhance their professional duty. Training is essential for them to take on the role of advocates, change agents, counsellors and guides.

The interplay with policymaker roles is evident when one considers that the implications discussed in Section 7.1 will require health care providers to widen their role from simply commanding to empowering patients to make their own informed decisions. This is only possible if patients understand their options and the respective benefits and harms. To do this, clinicians' communication skills and sensitivity to culture, gender and age differences should be promoted, along with training to foster the reciprocal exchange of knowledge, relationship-building, cooperative definition of targets and adoption of habits, especially for patients with a chronic disease. National health agencies (e.g. the National Health Service (NHS) in the United Kingdom (UK)) and health insurance companies can provide stimuli to support health literacy. Patient or consumer organisations may promote engagement and health literacy-friendly settings. Integrating patients or opinion leaders in the conception and implementation of quality improvement measures can render health care organisations more health literacy-friendly and assist in the shift towards patient-centredness. European patient organisations and other networks may prove influential partners to foster health literacy and enhance patient care. Health literacy should be tackled by policymakers as a challenge to society, systems, organisations and agencies (WHO, 2013).

Health care organisations and managers should establish practical strategies for promoting health literacy in clinical practice for health care staff. Such strategies can be categorised by whether they refer to verbal communication, written communication, visual aids or whether they support patient self-management and empowerment or supportive systems and caring environments.

7.2.2 Verbal Communication

The Agency for Healthcare Research and Quality (2020) reports that making assumptions about patients' language preferences or literacy levels should be avoided and that patients' preferred languages should be confirmed by asking the patient. The Institute of Medicine Roundtable on Health Literacy (2012) concurs that universal precautions are best practices that should be applied consistently to enhance communication and engagement for individuals at all health literacy levels. Smith and Magnani (2019) found that health care organisations should identify universal precautions of digital health literacy to increase accessibility for users who may be able to take advantage of eHealth offerings. An overview of universal digital precautions to promote eHealth is given in Section 7.2.8. Health professional staff should be encouraged to use understandable, jargon-free language, to speak clearly and slowly (Schillinger et al., 2004; Parnell et al., 2014). Content should be limited (Agency for Healthcare Research and Quality 2020; Schillinger et al., 2004), otherwise only partial information will be retained. The critical information should be repeated and confirmed more than once to support patient understanding and learning. To do this, the teach-back method can be applied, where the patient is asked to describe a topic or a treatment plan in their own words to ensure it was conveyed clearly. Alternatively, the 'chunk and check' method is used, where the health care professional stops after each key point and asks whether the patient has questions and then has the patient explain the same point (Hersh et al., 2015; Agency for Healthcare Research and Quality, 2020).

7.2.3 Written Communication

Written material fosters understanding by reinforcing verbal communication. Easy-to-read material (5th- or 6th-grade reading level) is preferred. Cajita et al. (2016) found that most consent forms that patients with heart failure encountered in their study were written at a 10th-grade reading level, which could discourage patients from participating in their health action plan. Patient-centred labelling in pharmacies focusses on guidelines to facilitate patient understanding of their prescription medication (Khoong et al., 2018). The content should be given in short sentences and short words (avoiding words with more than two syllables) and limited to the most relevant information. Medical jargon should be avoided, and if used, terms should be defined. The information should be structured and chunked into sections; the information should be reviewed together with patient and key points marked.

If patients have to fill in forms, checking boxes will often be more manageable than writing open answers and 'I don't know' should be a possible option. Highlighting the central theme/word of a sentence in bold may also be advantageous. Tools to help health care organisations and health care professionals are electronic assessment tools to determine whether the reading level of the written material is comprehensible (Hersh et al., 2015).

7.2.4 Numerical Information

Numerical information plays an essential role in communicating health information; however, studies show that most people, not only those with limited health literacy, have difficulty understanding numerical concepts such as percentage (Apter et al., 2006). Cognitive theory indicates that the way in which numerical data are presented and framed can influence how we perceive it. Readers are referred to Hersh et al. (2015) for a review of strategies that address limited numeracy.

7.2.5 Visual Aids

Visual aids can be beneficial, especially when added to other forms of communication; simple pictures are preferable (Garcia-Retamero & Galesic, 2010). Models, photonovelas, i.e. easy-to-read stories formatted similar to comics but with photos instead of drawings, and videos are also useful. Patients with internet access can search for illustrative, informative and entertaining multimedia online (e.g. YouTube) (Hersh et al., 2015).

7.2.6 Patient Self-Management and Empowerment

Patients should be encouraged to participate by formulating questions such as 'What questions do you have?' rather than 'Do you have any questions?' or by encouraging them to bring two or three questions to doctor appointments. Understanding medications and adherence should be assessed by asking how patients remember to take their medications. When giving instructions, preciseness may be helpful, e.g. specifying the time when medications should be taken rather than instructing patients to take them twice daily and suggesting tools for organising the medications, such as pillboxes. Medication should also be reviewed at all encounters, and general feedback elicited. To involve the patient and render the process more transparent, an action plan delineating the patient's steps to achieve targets should be set forth. Helpful tools are the 'brown bag' review of medications, in which patients are asked to bring with them to the appointment all the medications and supplements they are currently taking. In this way, what is being taken can be verified, questions answered and adherence improved. Patients should also be encouraged to remember three things before leaving the encounter: the problem that brought them to seek medical attention, what they need to do and why they should act accordingly. Patients can be asked to repeat these three points back to the health care professional, so as to assure they have been understood (Hersh et al., 2015).

7.2.7 Supportive Systems and Caring Environments

To create a supportive ecosystem, patients can be referred to nonmedical support and health and literacy resources; all referrals should be accompanied by clear instructions and reviewed with the patient. Staff should be made aware of and trained in health literacy and communication. Simple forms with understandable language should be applied and help offered, but paperwork should be generally limited. Tools are presented by the Agency for Healthcare Research and Quality Health Literacy Universal Precautions Toolkit (http://www.ah rq.gov/professionals/qualitypatient-safety/quality-resources/to ols/literacy-toolkit/index.html). Readers are referred to Hersh et al. (2015) for a review of communication techniques and strategies.

7.2.8 Steps to Promote eHealth and Electronic Health Literacy

The following steps are adapted from Smith and Magnani (2019).

1. Form a multidisciplinary team of providers, designers, programmers and patients

2. Identify opportunities by determining which care systems can be improved with digital technology

3. Develop a health literacy standard for material and tools in line with universal precautions

4. Offer understandable content that is clear, concise and easy for patients to act upon

5. Assess readability to ensure materials are accessible for everyone (e.g. avoid jargon)

6. Promote intuitive designs that are easily navigable

7. Enhance communication with multimedia to include individuals with low general literacy

8. Present information in context to ensure explanations and test results are understandable and solicit questions

9. Facilitate understanding by providing access to additional information

10. Tailor information so that it is adapted to patient experience

11. Focus on ease of use, minimise time- or work-intensive features

12. Determine access to technology and a patient's available and preferred communication channels

13. Provide means to access services for patients who do not have them

14. Encourage patient participation by advertising services and incentivising their use

15. Offer technical support by designating employees to support patients during the use of eHealth services

16. Recommend helpful (evidence-based) devices, such as fitness trackers or pillbox apps

17. Solicit patient feedback by encouraging patients to evaluate services and suggest improvements

18. Share the results of interventions and their efficacy

Many of these suggestions align with what was suggested earlier in this section. Finally, the implementation of eHealth can facilitate understanding.

7.3 OVERVIEW AND SUMMARY OF IMPLICATIONS AND LESSONS

The implications and lessons for policymakers and health care managers are summarised in Table 1. They were categorised by whether they regard the health care and health literacy environment or a specific industry sector and are labelled 'environment' in the column 'extent' and 'granular', respectively. The columns 'P' and 'H' refer to whether the implication primarily involves the responsibility of policymakers (P) or health care managers and professionals. The various spheres of health literacy are interrelated; the classification is fluid and reflects the 'big picture'. A short title of the implications and a description are presented. Exemplary initiatives and an estimation of the implication's impact are listed in the 'Cases and Impact' column.

The implications 'Health and Health Literacy as a Public Good', 'Advocacy and Leadership' and 'Acute Need for Data' were labelled prerequisites since, without them, health literacy initiatives would likely not exist, not be effective or not elicit meaningful action. 'Collaborate' is vital to facilitate and speed up progress; however, health literacy programmes may be implemented even when there is still room for improvement. 'Communication and media', 'education', 'marketplace and communities' and 'health-literate organisations' were deemed action areas of high impact due to the number of successful initiatives encountered in these spheres. 'Patient self-management and empowerment', 'supportive systems and caring environments' and 'digital information' were classified as having a medium but growing impact. These implications are garnering more and more prominence and are most closely linked to the 'new normal' of health care and recent trends in patient behaviour. Patient-centredness and empowerment are only feasible when patients are health

Table 1. Implications and Lessons.

Extent	P	H	Short Title	Content	Cases and Impact
Environment	✓	✓	Health and HL as Public Good	Health-related rights and access to health information are crucial to reduce health inequalities and safeguard sustainable health care systems; provide help in navigating health care systems; include vulnerable groups and high-risk situations; health-literate organisations and health care professionals are a vital part	MiMi Project in Germany for Migrants (Salman & Weyers, 2010; WHO Health Evidence Network, 2019) *Prerequisite*
Environment	✓	✓	Advocacy and Leadership	Acknowledge importance of HL; actively promote, develop and implement HL initiatives; leadership should actively participate; introduce standards and agencies; integrate HL into evaluation measures and quality control	(Dowrick et al., 2013; Mabachi et al., 2016) stressed acknowledgement and leadership initiatives in settings; establishment of ÖPGK (Austrian platform for HL) (Bundesgesundheitsagentur, 2015; WHO Health Evidence Network, 2019) *Prerequisite*

Table 1. (*Continued*)

Extent	P	H	Short Title	Content	Cases and Impact
Environment	✓	✓	Acute Need for Data	More research should be conducted on initiatives, measurement tools and indicators; draw up a validated evaluation framework	(Walker et al., 2020; WHO Health Evidence Network, 2019) stress gaps in evidence *Prerequisite*
Environment	✓	✓	Collaborate	Working together and sharing results and best practices can accelerate progress; incorporate feedback from targeted population sub-groups in design, implementation and evaluation without stigmatising	Partnership and coordination in the MiMi Project (Salman & Weyers, 2010) *Facilitating factor*
Granular	✓	✓	Communication and Media	Support providers of public health information; enhance public health communication and its quality; counter misinformation; communicate clearly in verbal, written and numerical information and visual aids	Warning labels on cigarette packets, public service announcements *High impact*
Granular		✓	Education	Early childhood education and lifelong learning ensure desirable HL results; apply best practices	Schools and impact (St. Leger, 2001), teaching and education interventions *High impact*

Granular				
Granular	✓	Marketplace and Communities	Support users and regulate the environment; safeguard the provision of reliable, easily understandable health information; meet people 'where they already go', and encourage healthy behaviour	Nudging, mandatory labelling of nutritional value and allergens on food products *High impact*
Granular	✓ ✓	Health Literate Organisations	Apply criteria of health-literate organisations and universal precautions; use HL strategies in communication and confirm understanding	Mabachi et al. (2016) estimated effects of health-literate health care organisations *High Impact*
Granular	✓	Patient Self-management and Empowerment	Encourage patients to participate; solicit feedback; use HL strategies and patient-centredness	Diabetes self-management (Micklethwaite et al., 2012) *Medium but growing impact*
Granular	✓ ✓	Supportive Systems and Caring Environments	Create a supportive ecosystem by training health care professionals; refer patients to other resources if necessary	Lay Health Educator Programme (Galiatsatos et al., 2015) *Medium but growing impact*
Granular	✓ ✓	Digital Information	Promote eHealth and EHL; apply HL standards and strategies to eHealth to facilitate understanding	Digital Universal Precautions (Smith & Magnani, 2019) *Medium but growing impact*

literate to some degree. Supportive and connected health care systems have the patient in their centre and are currently being developed and strengthened. Digital sources of health information are increasingly used; however, not all the information on the internet is from trusted sources. Trends in internet use were discussed in Section 3.1.

The various different spheres of action interact with one another and may mutually reinforce each other's impact. A multilateral approach is essential.

8

WHAT WE SHOULD KNOW AND CONCLUSIONS

Although health literacy as a concept has been around since the 1970s, research gaps concerning the effects of initiatives, such as long-term effectiveness and cost-effectiveness analysis and implementation of its results, remain. The short-term effectiveness of some interventions has been documented, but studies examining whether these effects last over a more extended period are relatively scarce. Despite the attention this topic has received, more research needs to go into how to help disadvantaged population groups, so as not to exacerbate existing disparities. Equity and accessibility are especially relevant for technological innovations and eHealth literacy since they may help to reduce disparities when tailored to the target audience. Though it is no easy goal to reach individuals with low health literacy, within the context of the 'new normal' of health care, technological innovation may facilitate centring the patient. The problem exists on a national, European and global level. More research needs to be directed towards reducing health disparities effectively (Chaudhry et al., 2011) and how to reach disadvantaged groups. To take full advantage of the benefits that health technology can offer, more research should be conducted to identify best practices to be incorporated into the care process (Conard, 2019).

While the relationship between health literacy and health outcomes has been studied for some conditions, for others an association has not been established and the association between
health literacy and self-efficacy, gender and the environment needs
to be better researched (Caruso et al., 2018). Zanchetta and
Poureslami (2006) addressed this partly in their study in which
they noted that there remain gaps in our knowledge about health
service access and utilisation by culturally diverse groups in terms
of gender, learning styles, methods of navigating the health care
system and help-seeking behaviour. Walker et al. (2020) share this
observation and report evidence gaps in initiatives addressing
secondary prevention, targeting disadvantaged and regional
populations, health professional capacity-building initiatives,
quality improvement and system support initiatives.

Furthermore, while scholars have acknowledged the need
to broaden the focus from individuals to community settings
(Rogers et al., 2014), studies are still predominantly conducted in health and education settings and primarily measure
health literacy at the individual level (WHO Health Evidence
Network, 2019). New research should align its focus with
how we observe and assess health literacy in community settings. Studies have applied health literacy conceptual models
for project or initiative evaluation; however, the WHO was
unable to identify any international, national or regional
health literacy evaluation framework in a systematic review
conducted in 2019 (WHO Health Evidence Network, 2019).
Such frameworks, if validated, may be helpful for researchers,
policymakers and health professionals since they could be
used to identify the dimension of health literacy and how to
evaluate outcomes. Furthermore, one may wish to include a
time lag in the data analysis, as health literacy may precede
desirable health outcomes because it may be necessary to be
health literate to obtain them. Conversely, one could argue
that people with worse health outcomes may be encouraged

by medical professionals or by their own motivation to improve their health or at least prevent illness by informing themselves, which may be a challenging course of action when burdened by sickness. In any case, data analysis with a positive or negative time lag may reveal new insights into how people manage their health.

The limitations to the present volume and the recommendations for future research include the datedness of the data. Recent health literacy data are challenging to obtain and, if available at all, exist only for single years in irregular time intervals. As mentioned in Section 7.1.3, the periodic measurement of health literacy (and eHealth literacy) is recommended by the WHO (WHO, 2013). If these data become available, renewed analysis of potential associations are recommended. With more data available, one could also evaluate differences between countries or subpopulations and focus on these aspects, which could be especially relevant when decision-makers deal with disadvantaged groups.

Another potential limitation is the reliance on self-reported eHealth literacy indicators, which, again, is to be attributed to the lack of other measures. As mentioned in Section 7.1.3, the WHO recommends developing new indicators, with which one could also safeguard the validity and reliability of measures, which may be limited in the survey results provided in this volume.

'Health literacy is linked to literacy and entails people's knowledge, motivation and competences to access, understand, appraise and apply health information in order to make judgements and take decisions in everyday life concerning health care, disease prevention and health promotion to maintain or improve quality of life during the life course' (Sørensen et al., 2012, p. 83). Despite evidence that low health literacy is linked to undesirable outcomes such as poorer mental and physical health, lower health care system cost-effectiveness and greater health inequalities, studies of people's health literacy in several member stataes of the European Union showed that almost half of all respondents exhibited limited health literacy.

In the context of 'the new normal' of health care, health literacy is a prerequisite for patient-centredness, co-creation, co-production and initiative medicine since only health literate patients can self-manage and take greater responsibility for their own health care, prevention and health promotion.

Where to obtain information and how it is communicated are central issues. While initiatives to improve health literacy vary widely in their setting, implementation and outcome, this volume has focussed on technological initiatives, their advantages and potential barriers to their use.

Building on the results of the qualitative literature review, implications for policymakers and health care managers were discussed. In conclusion, it can be said that the relationship between the 'new normal' of health care and health literacy is mutually reinforcing. Health literacy is a prerequisite for patient-centredness and greater patient involvement and empowerment. However, 'the new normal' of health care and its directions for health policymaking and management may provide a suitable setting for health-literate health organisations and fostering health literacy and eHealth literacy.

ANNEX A: ARTICLES INCLUDED IN THE SYSTEMATIC REVIEW

Aaby, A., Friis, K., Christensen, B., & Maindal, H. T. (2020). Health literacy among people in cardiac rehabilitation: Associations with participation and health-related quality of life in the heart skills study in Denmark. *International Journal of Environmental Research and Public Health*, *17*(2). https://doi.org/10.3390/ijerph17020443

Aaby, A., Simonsen, C. B., Ryom, K., & Maindal, H. T. (2020). Improving organizational health literacy responsiveness in cardiac rehabilitation using a co-design methodology: Results from the heart skills study. *International Journal of Environmental Research and Public Health*, *17*(3). https://doi.org/10.3390/ijerph17031015

Abel, K. M., Bee, P., Gega, L., Gellatly, J., Kolade, A., Hunter, D., Callender, C., Carter, L.-A., Meacock, R., Bower, P., Stanley, N., Calam, R., Wolpert, M., Stewart, P., Emsley, R., Holt, K., Linklater, H., Douglas, S., Stokes-Crossley, B., & Green, J. (2020). An intervention to improve the quality of life in children of parents with serious mental illness: The young SMILES feasibility RCT. *Health Technology Assessment*, *24*(59), 1–136. https://doi.org/10.3310/hta24590

Adepoju, O., Mask, A., & McLeod, A. (2018). Health insurance literacy as a determinant of population health. *Population Health Management*, 21(2), 85–87. https://doi.org/10.1089/pop.2017.0078

Aguirre Velasco, A., Cruz, I. S. S., Billings, J., Jimenez, M., & Rowe, S. (2020). What are the barriers, facilitators and interventions targeting help-seeking behaviours for common mental health problems in adolescents? A systematic review. *BMC Psychiatry*, 20(1), 293. https://doi.org/10.1186/s12888-020-02659-0

Ahmed, T., Rizvi, S. J. R., Rasheed, S., Iqbal, M., Bhuiya, A., Standing, H., Bloom, G., & Waldman, L. (2020). Digital health and inequalities in access to health services in Bangladesh: Mixed methods study. *JMIR mHealth and uHealth*, 8(7), e16473. https://doi.org/10.2196/16473

Akin-Akinyosoye, K., Sarmanova, A., Fernandes, G. S., Frowd, N., Swaithes, L., Stocks, J., Valdes, A., McWilliams, D. F., Zhang, W., Doherty, M., Ferguson, E., & Walsh, D. A. (2020). Baseline self-report 'central mechanisms' trait predicts persistent knee pain in the Knee Pain in the Community (KPIC) cohort. *Osteoarthritis and Cartilage*, 28(2), 173–181. https://doi.org/10.1016/j.joca.2019.11.004

Akter, S., Doran, F., Avila, C., & Nancarrow, S. (2014). A qualitative study of staff perspectives of patient non-attendance in a regional primary healthcare setting. *The Australasian Medical Journal*, 7(5), 218–226. https://doi.org/10.4066/AMJ.2014.2056

Alameddine, M., AlGurg, R., Otaki, F., & Alsheikh-Ali, A. A. (2020). Physicians' perspective on shared decision-making in Dubai: A cross-sectional study. *Human Resources for Health*, 18(1), 33. https://doi.org/10.1186/s12960-020-00475-x

Alangari, A. S., Knox, S. S., Kristjansson, A. L., Wen, S., Innes, K. E., Bilal, L., Alhabeeb, A., Al-Subaie, A. S., & Altwaijri, Y. A. (2020). Barriers to mental health treatment in the Saudi National Mental Health Survey. *International Journal of Environmental Research and Public Health*, 17(11). https://doi.org/10.3390/ijerph17113877

Almunawar, M. N., Wint, Z., Low, K. C. P., & Anshari, M. (2012). Customer expectation of e-health systems in Brunei Darussalam. *Journal of Health Care Finance*, 38(4), 36–49.

Alsem, M. W., van Meeteren, K. M., Verhoef, M., Schmitz, M. J. W. M., Jongmans, M. J., Meily-Visser, J. M. A., & Ketelaar, M. (2017). Co-creation of a digital tool for the empowerment of parents of children with physical disabilities. *Research Involvement and Engagement*, 3, 26. https://doi.org/10.1186/s40900-017-0079-6

Alvarado-Little, W. (2020). Health literacy initiatives and lessons learned within public health agencies. *Studies in Health Technology and Informatics*, 269, 294–302. https://doi.org/10.3233/SHTI200044

Amarasuriya, S. D., Jorm, A. F., & Reavley, N. J. (2015). Quantifying and predicting depression literacy of undergraduates: A cross sectional study in Sri Lanka. *BMC Psychiatry*, 15, 269. https://doi.org/10.1186/s12888-015-0658-8

Ammentorp, J., Bigi, S., Silverman, J., Sator, M., Gillen, P., Ryan, W., Rosenbaum, M., Chiswell, M., Doherty, E., & Martin, P. (2021). Upscaling communication skills training – Lessons learned from international initiatives. *Patient Education and Counseling*, 104(2), 352–359. https://doi.org/10.1016/j.pec.2020.08.028

Andresen, M.-L., Rosof, B. M., & Arteaga, H. (2020). Achieving the quadruple aim through bidirectional care. *Studies in Health Technology and Informatics, 269*, 52–64. https://doi.org/10.3233/SHTI200022

Anshari, M., Almunawar, M. N., Low, P. K. C., Wint, Z., & Younis, M. Z. (2013). Adopting customers' empowerment and social networks to encourage participations in e-health services. *Journal of Health Care Finance, 40*(2), 17–41.

Aspden, T., Wolley, M. J., Ma, T. M., Rajah, E., Curd, S., Kumar, D., Lee, S., Pireva, K., Taule'alo, O., Tiavale, P., Kam, A. L., Suh, J. S., Kennedy, J., & Marshall, M. R. (2015). Understanding barriers to optimal medication management for those requiring long-term dialysis: Rationale and design for an observational study, and a quantitative description of study variables and data. *BMC Nephrology, 16*, 102. https://doi.org/10.1186/s12882-015-0097-2

Atilola, O. (2016). Mental health service utilization in Sub-Saharan Africa: Is public mental health literacy the problem? Setting the perspectives right. *Global Health Promotion, 23*(2), 30–37. https://doi.org/10.1177/1757975914567179

Attygalle, U. R., Perera, H., & Jayamanne, B. D. W. (2017). Mental health literacy in adolescents: Ability to recognise problems, helpful interventions and outcomes. *Child and Adolescent Psychiatry and Mental Health, 11*, 38. https://doi.org/10.1186/s13034-017-0176-1

Austvoll-Dahlgren, A., Oxman, A. D., Chalmers, I., Nsangi, A., Glenton, C., Lewin, S., Morelli, A., Rosenbaum, S., Semakula, D., & Sewankambo, N. (2015). Key concepts that people need to understand to assess claims about treatment effects. *Journal of Evidence-Based Medicine, 8*(3), 112–125. https://doi.org/10.1111/jebm.12160

Austvoll-Dahlgren, A., Semakula, D., Nsangi, A., Oxman, A. D., Chalmers, I., Rosenbaum, S., & Guttersrud, Ø. (2017). Measuring ability to assess claims about treatment effects: The development of the 'claim evaluation tools'. *BMJ Open*, 7(5), e013184. https://doi.org/10.1136/bmjopen-2016-013184

Bailey, S. C., Wolf, M. S., Lopez, A., Russell, A., Chen, A. H., Schillinger, D., Moy, G., & Sarkar, U. (2014). Expanding the universal medication schedule: A patient-centred approach. *BMJ Open*, 4(1), e003699. https://doi.org/10.1136/bmjopen-2013-003699

Bala, S., Keniston, A., & Burden, M. (2020). Patient perception of plain-language medical notes generated using artificial intelligence software: Pilot mixed-methods study. *JMIR Formative Research*, 4(6), e16670. https://doi.org/10.2196/16670

Barr, P. J., Forcino, R. C., Dannenberg, M. D., Mishra, M., Turner, E., Zisman-Ilani, Y., Matthews, J., Hinn, M., Bruce, M., & Elwyn, G. (2019). Healthcare Options for People Experiencing Depression (HOPE*D): The development and pilot testing of an encounter-based decision aid for use in primary care. *BMJ Open*, 9(4), e025375. https://doi.org/10.1136/bmjopen-2018-025375

Batterham, R. W., Buchbinder, R., Beauchamp, A., Dodson, S., Elsworth, G. R., & Osborne, R. H. (2014). The OPtimising HEalth LIterAcy (Ophelia) process: Study protocol for using health literacy profiling and community engagement to create and implement health reform. *BMC Public Health*, 14, 694. https://doi.org/10.1186/1471-2458-14-694

Beauchamp, A., Mohebbi, M., Cooper, A., Pridmore, V., Livingston, P., Scanlon, M., Davis, M., O'Hara, J., & Osborne, R. (2020). The impact of translated reminder letters and phone calls on mammography screening booking rates:

Two randomised controlled trials. *PLoS One*, *15*(1), e0226610. https://doi.org/10.1371/journal.pone.0226610

Behnke, L. M., Solis, A., Shulman, S. A., & Skoufalos, A. (2013). A targeted approach to reducing overutilization: Use of percutaneous coronary intervention in stable coronary artery disease. *Population Health Management*, *16*(3), 164–168. https://doi.org/10.1089/pop.2012.0019

Bellander, T., & Karlsson, A.-M. (2019). Patient participation and learning in medical consultations about congenital heart defects. *PLoS One*, *14*(7), e0220136. https://doi.org/10.1371/journal.pone.0220136

Benis, A., Tamburis, O., Chronaki, C., & Moen, A. (2021). One digital health: A unified framework for future health ecosystems. *Journal of Medical Internet Research*, *23*(2), e22189. https://doi.org/10.2196/22189

Betz, C. L., Ruccione, K., Meeske, K., Smith, K., & Chang, N. (2008). Health literacy: A pediatric nursing concern. *Pediatric Nursing*, *34*(3), 231–239.

Bircher, J., & Hahn, E. G. (2017). Will the Meikirch model, a new framework for health, induce a paradigm shift in healthcare? *Cureus*, *9*(3), e1081. https://doi.org/10.7759/cureus.1081

Birkenhead, G., & Grant, M. J. (2012). Informing the public health. *Health Information and Libraries Journal*, *29*(3), 177–179. https://doi.org/10.1111/j.1471-1842.2012.00998.x

Blitz, J., Swisher, J., & Sweitzer, B. (2020). Special considerations related to race, sex, gender, and socioeconomic status in the preoperative evaluation: Part 1: Race, history of incarceration, and health literacy. *Anesthesiology Clinics*, *38*(2), 247–261. https://doi.org/10.1016/j.anclin.2020.01.005

Booth, A. (2011). Evidence-based practice: Triumph of style over substance? *Health Information and Libraries Journal*, 28(3), 237–241. https://doi.org/10.1111/j.1471-1842.2011.00949.x

Bousquet, J. J., Schünemann, H. J., Togias, A., Erhola, M., Hellings, P. W., Zuberbier, T., Agache, I., Ansotegui, I. J., Anto, J. M., Bachert, C., Becker, S., Bedolla-Barajas, M., Bewick, M., Bosnic-Anticevich, S., Bosse, I., Boulet, L. P., Bourrez, J. M., Brusselle, G., Chavannes, N., & Zidarn, M. (2019). Next-generation ARIA care pathways for rhinitis and asthma: A model for multimorbid chronic diseases. *Clinical and Translational Allergy*, 9, 44. https://doi.org/10.1186/s13601-019-0279-2

Bowskill, D., & Garner, L. (2012). Medicines non-adherence: Adult literacy and implications for practice. *British Journal of Nursing*, 21(19), 1156–1159. https://doi.org/10.12968/bjon.2012.21.19.1156

Bramsved, R., Regber, S., Novak, D., Mehlig, K., Lissner, L., & Mårild, S. (2018). Parental education and family income affect birthweight, early longitudinal growth and body mass index development differently. *Acta Paediatrica*, 107(11), 1946–1952. https://doi.org/10.1111/apa.14215

Brian, R. M., & Ben-Zeev, D. (2014). Mobile health (mHealth) for mental health in Asia: Objectives, strategies, and limitations. *Asian Journal of Psychiatry*, 10, 96–100. https://doi.org/10.1016/j.ajp.2014.04.006

Brown, W., Balyan, R., Karter, A. J., Crossley, S., Semere, W., Duran, N. D., Lyles, C., Liu, J., Moffet, H. H., Daniels, R., McNamara, D. S., & Schillinger, D. (2021). Challenges and solutions to employing natural language processing and machine learning to measure patients' health literacy and physician writing complexity: The ECLIPPSE study. *Journal of Biomedical Informatics, 113*, 103658. https://doi.org/10.1016/j.jbi.2020.103658

Brown, J., Luderowski, A., Namusisi-Riley, J., Moore-Shelley, I., Bolton, M., & Bolton, D. (2020). Can a community-led intervention offering social support and health education improve maternal health? A repeated measures evaluation of the PACT project run in a socially deprived London borough. *International Journal of Environmental Research and Public Health, 17*(8). https://doi.org/10.3390/ijerph17082795

Calzone, K. A., Kirk, M., Tonkin, E., Badzek, L., Benjamin, C., & Middleton, A. (2018). Increasing nursing capacity in genomics: Overview of existing global genomics resources. *Nurse Education Today, 69*, 53–59. https://doi.org/10.1016/j.nedt.2018.06.032

Casamassimo, P. S., Lee, J. Y., Marazita, M. L., Milgrom, P., Chi, D. L., & Divaris, K. (2014). Improving children's oral health: An interdisciplinary research framework. *Journal of Dental Research, 93*(10), 938–942. https://doi.org/10.1177/0022034514547273

Cashman, S. B., & Seifer, S. D. (2008). Service-learning: An integral part of undergraduate public health. *American Journal of Preventive Medicine, 35*(3), 273–278. https://doi.org/10.1016/j.amepre.2008.06.012

Chapman, L. W., Ochoa, A., Tenconi, F., & Herman, A. (2015). Dermatologic health literacy in underserved communities: A case report of South Los Angeles Middle Schools. *Dermatology Online Journal, 21*(11), 13030.

Chen, Y., & Chalmers, I. (2015). Testing treatments interactive (TTi): Helping to equip the public to promote better research for better health care. *Journal of*

Evidence-Based Medicine, 8(2), 98–102. https://doi.org/10.1111/jebm.12155

Chiarelli, L., & Edwards, P. (2006). Building healthy public policy. *Canadian Journal of Public Health/Revue Canadienne De Sante Publique, 97*(Suppl. 2), S37–S42.

Chittamuru, D., Daniels, R., Sarkar, U., & Schillinger, D. (2020). Evaluating values-based message frames for type 2 diabetes prevention among Facebook audiences: Divergent values or common ground? *Patient Education and Counseling.* https://doi.org/10.1016/j.pec.2020.08.042

Coll-Planas, L., Blancafort, S., Rojano, X., Roqué, M., & Monteserín, R. (2018). Promoting self-management, health literacy and social capital to reduce health inequalities in older adults living in urban disadvantaged areas: Protocol of the randomised controlled trial AEQUALIS. *BMC Public Health, 18*(1), 345. https://doi.org/10.1186/s12889-018-5219-x

Copeland, L. A., Zeber, J. E., Thibodeaux, L. V., McIntyre, R. T., Stock, E. M., & Hochhalter, A. K. (2018). Postdischarge correlates of health literacy among medicaid inpatients. *Population Health Management, 21*(6), 493–500. https://doi.org/10.1089/pop.2017.0095

Cordier, R., & Wilson, N. J. (2014). Community-based men's sheds: Promoting male health, wellbeing and social inclusion in an international context. *Health Promotion International, 29*(3), 483–493. https://doi.org/10.1093/heapro/dat033

Costa, A., Mourão, S., Santos, O., Alarcão, V., Virgolino, A., Nogueira, P., Bettencourt, M. R., Reis, S., Graça, A., & Henriques, A. (2021). I-DECIDE: A social prescribing and digital intervention protocol to promote sexual and reproductive health and quality of life among young Cape Verdeans. *International Journal of Environmental Research and Public Health*, *18*(3). https://doi.org/10.3390/ijerph18030850

Coughlan, D., Sahm, L., & Byrne, S. (2012). The importance of health literacy in the development of 'self care' cards for community pharmacies in Ireland. *Pharmacy Practice*, *10*(3), 143–150. https://doi.org/10.4321/s1886-36552012000300004

Crosswell, L. H. (2020). The doctor in my pocket: Examining mobile approaches to personal wellbeing. *Perspectives in Public Health*, *140*(2), 93–101. https://doi.org/10.1177/1757913918823808

Cusack, L., Del Mar, C. B., Chalmers, I., Gibson, E., & Hoffmann, T. C. (2018). Educational interventions to improve people's understanding of key concepts in assessing the effects of health interventions: A systematic review. *Systematic Reviews*, *7*(1), 68. https://doi.org/10.1186/s13643-018-0719-4

Cyril, S., Green, J., Nicholson, J. M., Agho, K., & Renzaho, A. M. N. (2016). Exploring service providers' perspectives in improving childhood obesity prevention among CALD communities in Victoria, Australia. *PLoS One*, *11*(10), e0162184. https://doi.org/10.1371/journal.pone.0162184

Cyril, S., Nicholson, J. M., Agho, K., Polonsky, M., & Renzaho, A. M. (2017). Barriers and facilitators to childhood obesity prevention among culturally and linguistically diverse (CALD) communities in Victoria, Australia. *Australian and New Zealand Journal of Public Health*, *41*(3), 287–293. https://doi.org/10.1111/1753-6405.12648

Dahl, M., Søndergaard, S. F., Diederichsen, A., Pouwer, F., Pedersen, S. S., Søndergaard, J., & Lindholt, J. (2021). Facilitating participation in cardiovascular preventive initiatives among people with diabetes: A qualitative study.

BMC Public Health, 21(1), 203. https://doi.org/10.1186/s12889-021-10172-6

Damus, K. (2008). Prevention of preterm birth: A renewed national priority. *Current Opinion in Obstetrics & Gynecology*, 20(6), 590–596. https://doi.org/10.1097/GCO.0b013e3283186964

Davis, T. C., Rademaker, A., Bennett, C. L., Wolf, M. S., Carias, E., Reynolds, C., Liu, D., & Arnold, C. L. (2014). Improving mammography screening among the medically underserved. *Journal of General Internal Medicine*, 29(4), 628–635. https://doi.org/10.1007/s11606-013-2743-3

Di Palo, K. E., Patel, K., Assafin, M., & Piña, I. L. (2017). Implementation of a patient navigator program to reduce 30-day heart failure readmission rate. *Progress in Cardiovascular Diseases*, 60(2), 259–266. https://doi.org/10.1016/j.pcad.2017.07.004

DiMascio, T. C., Zhen-Duan, J., Rabin, J., Vaughn, L. M., & Jacquez, F. (2020). Intercultural differences in healthcare experiences of Latinos in a nontraditional destination area. *Families, Systems & Health*, 38(3), 232–241. https://doi.org/10.1037/fsh0000516

Dirmaier, J., & Härter, M. (2011). Stärkung der Selbstbeteiligung in der Rehabilitation [Strengthening patient involvement in rehabilitation]. *Bundesgesundheitsblatt – Gesundheitsforschung – Gesundheitsschutz*, 54(4), 411–419. https://doi.org/10.1007/s00103-011-1243-z

DiSantostefano, R. L., Beck, M., Yeakey, A. M., Raphiou, I., & Stempel, D. A. (2014). Patient comprehension of medication guides for asthma and chronic obstructive pulmonary disease medications. *Therapeutic Innovation &*

Regulatory Science, 48(5), 574–582. https://doi.org/10.1177/2168479014524407

Dowrick, C., Chew-Graham, C., Lovell, K., Lamb, J., Aseem, S., Beatty, S., Bower, P., Burroughs, H., Clarke, P., Edwards, S., Gabbay, M., Gravenhorst, K., Hammond, J., Hibbert, D., Kovandžić, M., Lloyd-Williams, M., Waheed, W., & Gask, L. (2013). Increasing equity of access to high-quality mental health services in primary care: A mixed-methods study. https://doi.org/10.3310/pgfar01020

Dubbin, L., Burke, N., Fleming, M., Thompson-Lastad, A., Napoles, T. M., Yen, I., & Shim, J. K. (2021). Social literacy: Nurses' contribution toward the co-production of self-management. *Global Qualitative Nursing Research*, 8. https://doi.org/10.1177/2333393621993451

Duggan, L., McCarthy, S., Curtis, L. M., Wolf, M. S., Noone, C., Higgins, J. R., O'Shea, S., & Sahm, L. J. (2014). Associations between health literacy and beliefs about medicines in an Irish obstetric population. *Journal of Health Communication*, 19(Suppl. 2), 106–114. https://doi.org/10.1080/10810730.2014.936570

Eickhorst, A., Schreier, A., Brand, C., Lang, K., Liel, C., Renner, I., Neumann, A., & Sann, A. (2016). Inanspruchnahme von Angeboten der Frühen Hilfen und darüber hinaus durch Psychosozial Belastete Eltern [Knowledge and use of different support programs in the context of early prevention in relation to family-related psychosocial burden]. *Bundesgesundheitsblatt – Gesundheitsforschung – Gesundheitsschutz*, 59(10), 1271–1280. https://doi.org/10.1007/s00103-016-2422-8

Ekblad, S. (2020). To increase mental health literacy and human rights among new-coming, low-educated mothers with experience of war: A culturally, tailor-made group health promotion intervention with participatory methodology addressing indirectly the children. *Frontiers in Psychiatry*, *11*, 611. https://doi.org/10.3389/fpsyt.2020.00611

Emmerton, L. M., Mampallil, L., Kairuz, T., McKauge, L. M., & Bush, R. A. (2012). Exploring health literacy competencies in community pharmacy. *Health Expectations: An International Journal of Public Participation in Health Care and Health Policy*, *15*(1), 12–22. https://doi.org/10.1111/j.1369-7625.2010.00649.x

Farokhi, M. R., Muck, A., Lozano-Pineda, J., Boone, S. L., & Worabo, H. (2018). Using interprofessional education to promote oral health literacy in a faculty-student collaborative practice. *Journal of Dental Education*, *82*(10), 1091–1097. https://doi.org/10.21815/JDE.018.110

Farrington, R. (2020). Consternation and complexity: Learning from people who seek asylum. *Education for Primary Care: An Official Publication of the Association of Course Organisers, National Association of GP Tutors, World Organisation of Family Doctors*, *31*(1), 2–6. https://doi.org/10.1080/14739879.2019.1704633

Fathy, C., Patel, S., Sternberg, P., & Kohanim, S. (2016). Disparities in adherence to screening guidelines for diabetic retinopathy in the United States: A comprehensive review and guide for future directions. *Seminars in Ophthalmology*, *31*(4), 364–377. https://doi.org/10.3109/08820538.2016.1154170

Ferdinand, K. C., Senatore, F. F., Clayton-Jeter, H., Cryer, D. R., Lewin, J. C., Nasser, S. A., Fiuzat, M., & Califf, R. M. (2017). Improving medication adherence in cardiometabolic disease: Practical and regulatory implications. *Journal of the American College of Cardiology*, *69*(4), 437–451. https://doi.org/10.1016/j.jacc.2016.11.034

Fernando, N., Suveendran, T., & de Silva, C. (2017). Decentralizing provision of mental health care in Sri Lanka. *WHO South-East Asia Journal of Public Health*, 6(1), 18–21. https://doi.org/10.4103/2224-3151.206159

Fillon, M. (2012). Dermatologists start skin cancer awareness initiative. *Journal of the National Cancer Institute*, 104(17), 1272. https://doi.org/10.1093/jnci/djs389

FitzGerald, J. M., & Poureslami, I. (2014). Chronic disease management: A proving ground for health literacy. *Population Health Management*, 17(6), 321–323. https://doi.org/10.1089/pop.2014.0078

Foster, J., Miller, L., Isbell, S., Shields, T., Worthy, N., & Dunlop, A. L. (2015). mHealth to promote pregnancy and interconception health among African-American women at risk for adverse birth outcomes: A pilot study. *mHealth*, 1, 20. https://doi.org/10.3978/j.issn.2306-9740.2015.12.01

Fredrick, C. M., Linskens, R. J., Schilling, M. A., Eggen, A. T., Strickland, R. A., & Jacobs, E. A. (2022). The cancer clear & simple story: Developing a cancer prevention curriculum for rural Wisconsin through a community partnership. *Journal of Cancer Education: The Official Journal of the American Association for Cancer Education*, 37(2), 338–342. https://doi.org/10.1007/s13187-020-01819-w

Friedberg, R. D., & Bayar, H. (2017). If it works for pills, can it work for skills? Direct-to-consumer social marketing of evidence-based psychological treatments. *Psychiatric Services*, 68(6), 621–623. https://doi.org/10.1176/appi.ps.201600153

Galiatsatos, P., Haapanen, K. A., Nelson, K., Park, A., Sherwin, H., Robertson, M., Sheets, K., & Hale, W. D. (2018). Sociodemographic factors associated with types of projects implemented by volunteer lay health educators in their congregations. *Journal of Religion and Health*, 57(5), 1771–1778. https://doi.org/10.1007/s10943-018-0669-0

Galiatsatos, P., Rios, R., Daniel Hale, W., Colburn, J. L., & Christmas, C. (2015). The lay health educator program: Evaluating the impact of this community health initiative on the medical education of resident physicians. *Journal of Religion and Health*, 54(3), 1148–1156. https://doi.org/10.1007/s10943-015-0028-3

Garcia, S. F., Hahn, E. A., & Jacobs, E. A. (2010). Addressing low literacy and health literacy in clinical oncology practice. *The Journal of Supportive Oncology*, 8(2), 64–69.

Gbadamosi, S. O., Eze, C., Olawepo, J. O., Iwelunmor, J., Sarpong, D. F., Ogidi, A. G., Patel, D., Oko, J. O., Onoka, C., & Ezeanolue, E. E. (2018). A patient-held smartcard with a unique identifier and an mHealth platform to improve the availability of prenatal test results in rural Nigeria: Demonstration study. *Journal of Medical Internet Research*, 20(1), e18. https://doi.org/10.2196/jmir.8716

Gellatly, J., Bee, P., Kolade, A., Hunter, D., Gega, L., Callender, C., Hope, H., & Abel, K. M. (2019). Developing an intervention to improve the health related quality of life in children and young people with serious parental mental illness. *Frontiers in Psychiatry*, 10, 155. https://doi.org/10.3389/fpsyt.2019.00155

Goldberg, L. R., & Crocombe, L. A. (2017). Advances in medical education and practice: Role of massive open online courses. *Advances in Medical Education and Practice*, 8, 603–609. https://doi.org/10.2147/AMEP.S115321

Goldney, R. D., & Fisher, L. J. (2008). Have broad-based community and professional education programs influenced mental health literacy and treatment seeking of those with major depression and suicidal ideation? *Suicide & Life-Threatening Behavior*, *38*(2), 129–142. https://doi.org/10.1521/suli.2008.38.2.129

Goss, H. R., McDermott, C., Hickey, L., Issartel, J., Meegan, S., Morrissey, J., Murrin, C., Peers, C., Smith, C., Spillane, A., & Belton, S. (2021). Understanding disadvantaged adolescents' perception of health literacy through a systematic development of peer vignettes. *BMC Public Health*, *21*(1), 593. https://doi.org/10.1186/s12889-021-10634-x

Gourevitch, M. N., Jay, M. R., Goldfrank, L. R., Mendelsohn, A. L., Dreyer, B. P., Foltin, G. L., Lipkin, M., & Schwartz, M. D. (2012). Training physician investigators in medicine and public health research. *American Journal of Public Health*, *102*(7), e39–e45. https://doi.org/10.2105/AJPH.2011.300486

Gregorio, D. I., DeChello, L. M., & Segal, J. (2008). Service learning within the University of Connecticut master of public health program. *Public Health Reports*, *123*(Suppl. 2)44–52. https://doi.org/10.1177/00333549081230S207

Guendelman, S., Broderick, A., Mlo, H., Gemmill, A., & Lindeman, D. (2017). Listening to communities: Mixed-method study of the engagement of disadvantaged mothers and pregnant women with digital health technologies. *Journal of Medical Internet Research*, *19*(7), e240. https://doi.org/10.2196/jmir.7736

Güner, M. D., & Ekmekci, P. E. (2019). A survey study evaluating and comparing the health literacy knowledge and communication skills used by nurses and physicians. *Inquiry: A Journal of Medical Care Organization, Provision and Financing*, *56*. https://doi.org/10.1177/0046958019865831

Guo, S., Yu, X., & Okan, O. (2020). Moving health literacy research and practice towards a vision of equity, precision and transparency. *International Journal of Environmental Research and Public Health*, *17*(20). https://doi.org/10.3390/ijerph17207650

Hämeen-Anttila, K. (2016). Strategic development of medicines information: Expanding key global initiatives. *Research in Social and Administrative Pharmacy: RSAP*, *12*(3), 535–540. https://doi.org/10.1016/j.sapharm.2015.07.001

Hanson, M. A., Gluckman, P. D., Ma, R. C. W., Matzen, P., & Biesma, R. G. (2012). Early life opportunities for prevention of diabetes in low and middle income countries. *BMC Public Health*, *12*, 1025. https://doi.org/10.1186/1471-2458-12-1025

Harper, W., Cook, S., & Makoul, G. (2007). Teaching medical students about health literacy: 2 Chicago initiatives. *American Journal of Health Behavior*, *31*(Suppl. 1), S111–S114. https://doi.org/10.5555/ajhb.2007.31.supp.S111

Haun, J., Luther, S., Dodd, V., & Donaldson, P. (2012). Measurement variation across health literacy assessments: Implications for assessment selection in research and practice. *Journal of Health Communication*, *17*(Suppl. 3), 141–159. https://doi.org/10.1080/10810730.2012.712615

Hay, R., Estrada, R., & Grossmann, H. (2011). Managing skin disease in resource-poor environments – The role of community-oriented training and control programs. *International Journal of Dermatology*, *50*(5), 558–563. https://doi.org/10.1111/j.1365-4632.2011.04954.x

Hillyer, G. C., Schmitt, K. M., Lizardo, M., Reyes, A., Bazan, M., Alvarez, M. C., Sandoval, R., Abdul, K., & Orjuela, M. A. (2017). Electronic communication channel use and health information source preferences among Latinos in Northern

Manhattan. *Journal of Community Health*, 42(2), 349–357. https://doi.org/10.1007/s10900-016-0261-z

Hillyer, G. C., Schmitt, K. M., Reyes, A., Cruz, A., Lizardo, M., Schwartz, G. K., & Terry, M. B. (2020). Community education to enhance the more equitable use of precision medicine in Northern Manhattan. *Journal of Genetic Counseling*, 29(2), 247–258. https://doi.org/10.1002/jgc4.1244

Hogan, T. P., Hill, J. N., Locatelli, S. M., Weaver, F. M., Thomas, F. P., Nazi, K. M., Goldstein, B., & Smith, B. M. (2016). Health information seeking and technology use among veterans with spinal cord injuries and disorders. *PM & R: The Journal of Injury, Function, and Rehabilitation*, 8(2), 123–130. https://doi.org/10.1016/j.pmrj.2015.06.443

Holland-Hart, D. M., Addis, S. M., Edwards, A., Kenkre, J. E., & Wood, F. (2019). Coproduction and health: Public and clinicians' perceptions of the barriers and facilitators. *Health Expectations: An International Journal of Public Participation in Health Care and Health Policy*, 22(1), 93–101. https://doi.org/10.1111/hex.12834

Howe, C. J., Adame, T., Lewis, B., & Wagner, T. (2020). Original research: Assessing Organizational Focus on Health Literacy in North Texas Hospitals. *The American Journal of Nursing*, 120(12), 24–33. https://doi.org/10.1097/01.NAJ.0000723424.47838.4d

Intawong, K., Olson, D., & Chariyalertsak, S. (2021). Application technology to fight the COVID-19 pandemic: Lessons learned in Thailand. *Biochemical and Biophysical Research Communications*, 538, 231–237. https://doi.org/10.1016/j.bbrc.2021.01.093

Jang, S. M., Parker, W. M., Pai, A. B., Jiang, R., & Cardone, K. E. (2020). Assessment of literacy and numeracy skills related to medication labels in patients on chronic in-center hemodialysis. *Journal of the American Pharmacists Association*, 60(6), 957–962.e1. https://doi.org/10.1016/j.japh.2020.07.010

Jarernsiripornkul, N., Chaipichit, N., Chumworathayi, P., & Krska, J. (2015). Management for improving patients' knowledge and understanding about drug allergy. *Pharmacy Practice*, 13(1), 513. https://doi.org/10.18549/pharmpract.2015.01.513

Jessup, R. L., & Buchbinder, R. (2018). What if I cannot choose wisely? Addressing suboptimal health literacy in our patients to reduce over-diagnosis and overtreatment. *Internal Medicine Journal*, 48(9), 1154–1157. https://doi.org/10.1111/imj.14025

Joe, J. R., Young, R. S., Moses, J., Knoki-Wilson, U., & Dennison, J. (2016). A collaborative case study: The office of native medicine. *American Indian & Alaska Native Mental Health Research*, 23(2), 50–63. https://doi.org/10.5820/aian.2302.2016.50

Johri, M., Subramanian, S. V., Sylvestre, M.-P., Dudeja, S., Chandra, D., Koné, G. K., Sharma, J. K., & Pahwa, S. (2015). Association between maternal health literacy and child vaccination in India: A cross-sectional study. *Journal of Epidemiology & Community Health*, 69(9), 849–857. https://doi.org/10.1136/jech-2014-205436

Katz, S. J., Wallner, L. P., Abrahamse, P. H., Janz, N. K., Martinez, K. A., Shumway, D. A., Hamilton, A. S., Ward, K. C., Resnicow, K. A., & Hawley, S. T. (2017). Treatment experiences of Latinas after diagnosis of breast cancer.

Cancer, *123*(16), 3022–3030. https://doi.org/10.1002/cncr.30702

Kenya, S., Lebron, C. N., Chang, A. Y. H., Li, H., Alonzo, Y. A., & Carrasquillo, O. (2015). A profile of Latinos with poorly controlled diabetes in South Florida. *Journal of Community Hospital Internal Medicine Perspectives*, *5*(2), 26586. https://doi.org/10.3402/jchimp.v5.26586

Khoong, E. C., Cherian, R., Smith, D. E., Schillinger, D., Wolf, M. S., & Sarkar, U. (2018). Implementation of patient-centered prescription labeling in a safety-net ambulatory care network. *American Journal of Health-System Pharmacy: AJHP: Official Journal of the American Society of Health-System Pharmacists*, *75*(16), 1227–1238. https://doi.org/10.2146/ajhp170821

King, D. M., Donley, T., Mbizo, J., Higgins, M., Langaigne, A., Middleton, E. J., & Stokes-Williams, C. (2019). The use of a community-based preconception peer health educator training intervention to improve preconception health knowledge. *Journal of Racial and Ethnic Health Disparities*, *6*(4), 686–700. https://doi.org/10.1007/s40615-019-00567-y

Knapp, C. (2006). Bronson methodist hospital: Journey to excellence in quality and safety. *Joint Commission Journal on Quality and Patient Safety*, *32*(10), 556–563. https://doi.org/10.1016/s1553-7250(06)32073-9

Kohler, I. V., Bandawe, C., Ciancio, A., Kämpfen, F., Payne, C. F., Mwera, J., Mkandawire, J., & Kohler, H.-P. (2020). Cohort profile: The mature adults cohort of the Malawi longitudinal study of families and health (MLSFH-MAC). *BMJ Open*, *10*(10), e038232. https://doi.org/10.1136/bmjopen-2020-038232

Koonrungsesomboon, N., Traivaree, C., Tiyapsane, C., & Karbwang, J. (2019). Improved parental understanding by an enhanced informed consent form: A randomized controlled study nested in a paediatric drug trial. *BMJ Open*, *9*(11), e029530. https://doi.org/10.1136/bmjopen-2019-029530

Kosicka, B., Deluga, A., Bąk, J., Chałdaś-Majdańska, J., Bieniak, M., Machul, M., Chrzan-Rodak, A., Jurek, K., & Dobrowolska, B. (2020). The level of health literacy of seniors living in eastern region of Poland. Preliminary study. *Healthcare*, *8*(3). https://doi.org/10.3390/healthcare8030277

Koury, S. T., Carlin-Menter, S., Dey-Rao, R., & Kelly, K. (2020). Gene annotation in high schools: Successful student pipeline and teacher professional development in bioscience using GENI-ACT. *Frontiers in Microbiology*, *11*, 578747. https://doi.org/10.3389/fmicb.2020.578747

Kura, S., Vince, J., & Crouch-Chivers, P. (2013). Male involvement in sexual and reproductive health in the Mendi district, Southern Highlands province of Papua New Guinea: A descriptive study. *Reproductive Health*, *10*, 46. https://doi.org/10.1186/1742-4755-10-46

Kurtz-Rossi, S., Schwartz, F., Alemayehu, G., Chang, P., & Rubin, D. (2020). Building health literacy coalitions and NGOs. *Studies in Health Technology and Informatics*, *269*, 258–263. https://doi.org/10.3233/SHTI200040

Lantos, Z., & Simon, J. (2018). The community health experience model-value generation from person-centered health transaction network. *Public Health Reviews*, *39*, 29. https://doi.org/10.1186/s40985-018-0105-8

Larsen, A. K., Holtermann, A., Mortensen, O. S., Punnett, L., Rod, M. H., & Jørgensen, M. B. (2015). Organizing workplace health literacy to reduce musculoskeletal pain and consequences. *BMC Nursing*, *14*, 46. https://doi.org/10.1186/s12912-015-0096-4

Larson, H. J., Lee, N., Rabin, K. H., Rauh, L., & Ratzan, S. C. (2020). Building confidence to CONVINCE. *Journal of Health Communication*, *25*(10), 838–842. https://doi.org/10.1080/10810730.2021.1884149

Lawn, S., Westwood, T., Jordans, S., & O'Connor, J. (2017). Support workers as agents for health behavior change: An Australian study of the perceptions of clients with complex needs, support workers, and care coordinators. *Gerontology & Geriatrics Education*, *38*(4), 496–516. https://doi.org/10.1080/02701960.2016.1165218

Lawson, E. H., Carreón, R., Veselovskiy, G., & Escarce, J. J. (2011). Collection of language data and services provided by health plans. *The American Journal of Managed Care*, *17*(12), e479–e487.

Lenferink, A., Frith, P., van der Valk, P., Buckman, J., Sladek, R., Cafarella, P., van der Palen, J., & Effing, T. (2013). A self-management approach using self-initiated action plans for symptoms with ongoing nurse support in patients with chronic obstructive pulmonary disease (COPD) and comorbidities: The COPE-III study protocol. *Contemporary Clinical Trials*, *36*(1), 81–89. https://doi.org/10.1016/j.cct.2013.06.003

Levin-Zamir, D., & Bertschi, I. (2018). Media health literacy, eHealth literacy, and the role of the social environment in context. *International Journal of Environmental Research and Public Health*, *15*(8). https://doi.org/10.3390/ijerph15081643

Levin-Zamir, D., Sorensen, K., Su, T. T., Sentell, T., Rowlands, G., Messer, M., Pleasant, A., Saboga Nunes, L., Lev-Ari, S., & Okan, O. (2021). Health promotion preparedness for health crises – A 'must' or 'nice to have'? Case studies and global lessons learned from the COVID-19 pandemic. *Global Health Promotion*, *28*(2), 27–37. https://doi.org/10.1177/1757975921998639

Lin, L. C., Ketkar, A., Achalu, P., Alqaderi, H., Diamond, S., Spero, L., Turton, B., & Sokal-Gutierrez, K. (2021). Oral health knowledge and practices in the Kaski District of Nepal. *Community Dental Health*, *38*(2), 105–111. https://doi.org/10.1922/CDH_00134Lin07

Liu, D. Y., Maki, A. W., Maitland, A., Meyer, E. R., Sorensen, J. S., & Galvin, S. (2020). Enhancing knowledge in informal settlements: Assessing health beliefs and behaviors in Nigeria: A cross-sectional survey assessment of perceptions, practices, and resources in underserved urban communities in Lagos. *Annals of Global Health*, *86*(1), 121. https://doi.org/10.5334/aogh.2648

Logan, R. A. (2007). Clinical, classroom, or personal education: Attitudes about health literacy. *Journal of the Medical Library Association: JMLA*, *95*(2), 127–137, e48. https://doi.org/10.3163/1536-5050.95.2.127

Loignon, C., Dupéré, S., Fortin, M., Ramsden, V. R., & Truchon, K. (2018). Health literacy – Engaging the community in the co-creation of meaningful health navigation services: A study protocol. *BMC Health Services Research*, *18*(1), 505. https://doi.org/10.1186/s12913-018-3315-3

Mabachi, N. M., Cifuentes, M., Barnard, J., Brega, A. G., Albright, K., Weiss, B. D., Brach, C., & West, D. (2016). Demonstration of the health literacy universal precautions toolkit: Lessons for quality improvement. *The Journal of Ambulatory Care Management*, *39*(3), 199–208. https://doi.org/10.1097/JAC.0000000000000102

Maggio, L. A., Willinsky, J. M., Costello, J. A., Skinner, N. A., Martin, P. C., & Dawson, J. E. (2020). Integrating Wikipedia editing into health professions education: A curricular inventory and review of the literature. *Perspectives on Medical Education*, *9*(6), 333–342. https://doi.org/10.1007/s40037-020-00620-1

Malloy-Weir, L. J., Charles, C., Gafni, A., & Entwistle, V. (2016). A review of health literacy: Definitions, interpretations, and implications for policy initiatives. *Journal of Public Health Policy*, *37*(3), 334–352. https://doi.org/10.1057/jphp.2016.18

Marshall, S., Sahm, L., & McCarthy, S. (2012). Health literacy in Ireland: Reading between the lines. *Perspectives in Public Health*, *132*(1), 31–38. https://doi.org/10.1177/1757913911431034

Mårtensson, L., & Hensing, G. (2012). Experiences of factors contributing to women's ability to make informed decisions about the process of rehabilitation and return to work: A focus group study. *Work*, *43*(2), 237–248. https://doi.org/10.3233/WOR-2012-1397

Matima, R., Murphy, K., Levitt, N. S., BeLue, R., & Oni, T. (2018). A qualitative study on the experiences and perspectives of public sector patients in cape town in managing the workload of demands of HIV and type 2 diabetes multimorbidity. *PLoS One*, *13*(3), e0194191. https://doi.org/10.1371/journal.pone.0194191

Mazmudar, R. S., Sheth, A., Tripathi, R., & Scott, J. F. (2021). Readability of online Spanish patient education materials in dermatology. *Archives of Dermatological Research*, *313*(3), 201–204. https://doi.org/10.1007/s00403-020-02036-7

McCrea, Z., Power, K., Kiersey, R., White, M., Breen, A., Murphy, S., Healy, L., Kearney, H., Dunleavy, B., O'Donoghue, S., Lambert, V., Delanty, N., Doherty, C., & Fitzsimons, M. (2021). Coproducing health and well-being in partnership with patients, families, and healthcare providers: A qualitative study exploring the role of an epilepsy patient portal. *Epilepsy and Behavior: E&B*, *115*, 107664. https://doi.org/10.1016/j.yebeh.2020.107664

Micklethwaite, A., Brownson, C. A., O'Toole, M. L., & Kilpatrick, K. E. (2012). The business case for a diabetes self-management intervention in A community general hospital. *Population Health Management*, *15*(4), 230–235. https://doi.org/10.1089/pop.2011.0051

Modenese, A., Loney, T., Ruggieri, F. P., Tornese, L., & Gobba, F. (2020). Sun protection habits and behaviors of a group of outdoor workers and students from the agricultural and construction sectors in North-Italy. *La Medicina del Lavoro*, *111*(2), 116–125. https://doi.org/10.23749/mdl.v111i2.8929

Mond, J., Slewa-Younan, S., Gabriela Uribe Guajardo, M., Mohammad, Y., Johnson, E., & Milosevic, D. (2021). Self-recognition of trauma-related psychopathology and help-seeking among resettled Iraqi refugees in Australia. *Transcultural Psychiatry*, *58*(2), 215–225. https://doi.org/10.1177/1363461520901635

Montagni, I., Langlois, E., Wittwer, J., & Tzourio, C. (2017). Co-creating and evaluating a web-app mapping real-world health care services for students: The servi-share protocol. *JMIR Research Protocols*, *6*(2), e24. https://doi.org/10.2196/resprot.6801

Morgan-Daniel, J., Goodman, X. Y., Franklin, S. G., Bartley, K., Noe, M. N., & Pionke, J. J. (2021). Medical library association diversity and inclusion task force report. *Journal of the Medical Library Association: JMLA*, *109*(1), 141–153. https://doi.org/10.5195/jmla.2021.1112

Morris, R. L., Soh, S.-E., Hill, K. D., Buchbinder, R., Lowthian, J. A., Redfern, J., Etherton-Beer, C. D., Hill, A.-M., Osborne, R. H., Arendts, G., & Barker, A. L. (2017). Measurement properties of the health literacy questionnaire (HLQ) among older adults who present to the emergency department after a fall: A Rasch analysis. *BMC Health Services Research*, *17*(1), 605. https://doi.org/10.1186/s12913-017-2520-9

Moskow, J. M., Cook, N., Champion-Lippmann, C., Amofah, S. A., & Garcia, A. S. (2016). Identifying opportunities in EHR to improve the quality of antibiotic allergy data. *Journal of the American Medical Informatics Association: JAMIA*, *23*(e1), e108–e112. https://doi.org/10.1093/jamia/ocv139

Mottl-Santiago, J., Fox, C. S., Pecci, C. C., & Iverson, R. (2013). Multidisciplinary collaborative development of a plain-language prenatal education book. *Journal of Midwifery & Women's Health*, *58*(3), 271–277. https://doi.org/10.1111/jmwh.12059

Murphy, K., Chuma, T., Mathews, C., Steyn, K., & Levitt, N. (2015). A qualitative study of the experiences of care and motivation for effective self-management among diabetic and hypertensive patients attending public sector primary health care services in South Africa. *BMC Health Services Research*, *15*, 303. https://doi.org/10.1186/s12913-015-0969-y

Muscat, D. M., Morony, S., Shepherd, H. L., Smith, S. K., Dhillon, H. M., Trevena, L., Hayen, A., Luxford, K., Nutbeam, D., & McCaffery, K. (2015). Development and field testing of a consumer shared decision-making training program for adults with low literacy. *Patient Education and Counseling*, *98*(10), 1180–1188. https://doi.org/10.1016/j.pec.2015.07.023

Musich, S., Wang, S. S., Kraemer, S., Hawkins, K., & Wicker, E. (2018). Purpose in life and positive health outcomes among older adults. *Population Health Management*, *21*(2), 139–147. https://doi.org/10.1089/pop.2017.0063

Mwaisaka, J., Gonsalves, L., Thiongo, M., Waithaka, M., Sidha, H., Alfred, O., Mukiira, C., & Gichangi, P. (2021). Young people's experiences using an on-demand mobile health sexual and reproductive health text message intervention in Kenya: Qualitative study. *JMIR mHealth and uHealth*, *9*(1), e19109. https://doi.org/10.2196/19109

Naccarella, L., Biuso, C., Jennings, A., & Patsamanis, H. (2019). Improving access to important recovery information for heart patients with low health literacy: Reflections on practice-based initiatives. *Australian Health Review: A Publication of the Australian Hospital Association*, *43*(3), 323–327. https://doi.org/10.1071/AH17270

Nahm, E.-S., Zhu, S., Bellantoni, M., Keldsen, L., Russomanno, V., Rietschel, M., Majid, T., Son, H., & Smith, L. (2019). The effects of a theory-based patient portal e-learning program for older adults with chronic illnesses. *Telemedicine Journal and e-Health: The Official Journal of the American Telemedicine Association*, *25*(10), 940–951. https://doi.org/10.1089/tmj.2018.0184

National Academies Press. (2016). *Relevance of health literacy to precision medicine: Proceedings of a workshop*. https://doi.org/10.17226/23592

National Academies Press (US). (2010). *The safe use initiative and health literacy: Workshop summary*. https://doi.org/10.17226/12975

National Academies Press (US). (2016). *Relevance of health literacy to precision medicine: Workshop in brief*. https://doi.org/10.17226/23538

Nguyen, J., Smith, L., Hunter, J., & Harnett, J. E. (2019). Conventional and complementary medicine health care practitioners' perspectives on interprofessional communication: A qualitative rapid review. *Medicina*, 55(10). https://doi.org/10.3390/medicina55100650

Nicholson, E., McDonnell, T., De Brún, A., Barrett, M., Bury, G., Collins, C., Hensey, C., & McAuliffe, E. (2020). Factors that influence family and parental preferences and decision making for unscheduled paediatric healthcare – Systematic review. *BMC Health Services Research*, 20(1), 663. https://doi.org/10.1186/s12913-020-05527-5

Okolie, F., South-Paul, J. E., & Watchko, J. F. (2020). Combating the hidden health disparity of kernicterus in black infants: A review. *JAMA Pediatrics*, 174(12), 1199–1205. https://doi.org/10.1001/jamapediatrics.2020.1767

Oman, K. S., Mancuso, M. P., Ceballos, K., Makic, M. F., & Fink, R. M. (2016). Mentoring clinical nurses to write for publication: Strategies for success. *The American Journal of Nursing*, 116(5), 48–55. https://doi.org/10.1097/01.NAJ.0000482966.46919.0f

Osborne, B., Kelly, P. J., Robinson, L. D., Ivers, R., Deane, F. P., & Larance, B. (2021). Facilitators and barriers to integrating physical health care during treatment for substance use: A socio-ecological analysis. *Drug and Alcohol Review*, 40(4), 607–616. https://doi.org/10.1111/dar.13197

Palmer, N. R., Shim, J. K., Kaplan, C. P., Schillinger, D., Blaschko, S. D., Breyer, B. N., & Pasick, R. J. (2020). Ethnographic investigation of patient-provider communication among African American men newly diagnosed with prostate cancer: A study protocol. *BMJ Open*, *10*(8), e035032. https://doi.org/10.1136/bmjopen-2019-035032

Palumbo, R. (2021). Leveraging organizational health literacy to enhance health promotion and risk prevention: A narrative and interpretive literature review. *The Yale Journal of Biology and Medicine*, *94*(1), 115–128.

Palumbo, R., Annarumma, C., Adinolfi, P., & Musella, M. (2016). The missing link to patient engagement in Italy. *Journal of Health, Organisation and Management*, *30*(8), 1183–1203. https://doi.org/10.1108/JHOM-01-2016-0011

Patel, P., Adebisi, Y. A., Steven, M., & Lucero-Prisno, D. E., III. (2020). Addressing COVID-19 in Malawi. *The Pan African Medical Journal*, *35*(Suppl. 2), 71. https://doi.org/10.11604/pamj.supp.2020.35.2.23960

Paul, M. P., Rigrod, P., Wingate, S., & Borsuk, M. E. (2015). A community-driven intervention in Tuftonboro, New Hampshire, succeeds in altering water testing behavior. *Journal of Environmental Health*, *78*(5), 30–39.

Pelikan, J. M., Straßmayr, C., & Ganahl, K. (2020). Health literacy measurement in general and other populations: Further initiatives and lessons learned in Europe (and beyond). *Studies in Health Technology and Informatics*, *269*, 170–191. https://doi.org/10.3233/SHTI200031

Pinto-Meza, A., Moneta, M. V., Alonso, J., Angermeyer, M. C., Bruffaerts, R., Caldas de Almeida, J. M., de Girolamo, G., de Graaf, R., Florescu, S., Kovess Masfety, V., O'Neill, S.,

Vassilev, S., & Haro, J. M. (2013). Social inequalities in mental health: Results from the EU contribution to the World Mental Health Surveys Initiative. *Social Psychiatry and Psychiatric Epidemiology*, *48*(2), 173–181. https://doi.org/10.1007/s00127-012-0536-3

Pizzarelli, S., Cammarano, R. R., Sampaolo, L., & Della Seta, M. (2019). New roles and challenges for health information specialists: Professional changes over the years. *Health Information and Libraries Journal*, *36*(1), 101–105. https://doi.org/10.1111/hir.12246

Poureslami, I., Rootman, I., Pleasant, A., & FitzGerald, J. M. (2016). The emerging role of health literacy in chronic disease management: The response to a call for action in Canada. *Population Health Management*, *19*(4), 230–231. https://doi.org/10.1089/pop.2015.0163

Price-Haywood, E. G., Harden-Barrios, J., Ulep, R., & Luo, Q. (2017). eHealth literacy: Patient engagement in identifying strategies to encourage use of patient portals among older adults. *Population Health Management*, *20*(6), 486–494. https://doi.org/10.1089/pop.2016.0164

Rasin-Waters, D., Abel, V., Kearney, L. K., & Zeiss, A. (2018). The integrated care team approach of the Department of Veterans Affairs (VA): Geriatric primary care. *Archives of Clinical Neuropsychology: The Official Journal of the National Academy of Neuropsychologists*, *33*(3), 280–289. https://doi.org/10.1093/arclin/acx129

Razavi, A. C., Dyer, A., Jones, M., Sapin, A., Caraballo, G., Nace, H., Dotson, K., Razavi, M. A., & Harlan, T. S. (2020). Achieving dietary sodium recommendations and atherosclerotic cardiovascular disease prevention through culinary medicine education. *Nutrients*, *12*(12). https://doi.org/10.3390/nu12123632

Reedtz, C., van Doesum, K., Signorini, G., Lauritzen, C., van Amelsvoort, T., van Santvoort, F., Young, A. H., Conus, P., Musil, R., Schulze, T., Berk, M., Stringaris, A., Piché, G., & de Girolamo, G. (2019). Promotion of wellbeing for children of parents with mental illness: A model protocol for research and intervention. *Frontiers in Psychiatry*, *10*, 606. https://doi.org/10.3389/fpsyt.2019.00606

Renzaho, A. M., Green, J., Smith, B. J., & Polonsky, M. (2018). Exploring factors influencing childhood obesity prevention among migrant communities in Victoria, Australia: A qualitative study. *Journal of Immigrant and Minority Health*, *20*(4), 865–883. https://doi.org/10.1007/s10903-017-0620-6

Rezaei Aghdam, A., Watson, J., Cliff, C., & Miah, S. J. (2020). Improving the theoretical understanding toward patient-driven health care innovation through online value cocreation: Systematic review. *Journal of Medical Internet Research*, *22*(4), e16324. https://doi.org/10.2196/16324

Robbins, B. W., McLaughlin, S., Finn, P. W., Spencer, A. L., & Coleman, D. L. (2020). Young adults: Addressing the health needs of a vulnerable population. *The American Journal of Medicine*, *133*(8), 999–1002. https://doi.org/10.1016/j.amjmed.2020.04.005

Rogers, E. A., Fine, S., Handley, M. A., Davis, H., Kass, J., & Schillinger, D. (2014). Development and early implementation of the bigger picture, a youth-targeted public health literacy campaign to prevent type 2 diabetes. *Journal of Health Communication*, *19*(Suppl. 2), 144–160. https://doi.org/10.1080/10810730.2014.940476

Rosen, D. L., Gifford, E. J., & Ashkin, E. A. (2019). Overwhelming need, insufficient health care for justice-involved North Carolinians. *North Carolina Medical*

Journal, 80(6), 339–343. https://doi.org/10.18043/ncm.80.6.339

Rozier, R. G. (2012). Oral health in North Carolina: Innovations, opportunities, and challenges. *North Carolina Medical Journal, 73*(2), 100–107.

Runk, L., Durham, J., Vongxay, V., & Sychareun, V. (2017). Measuring health literacy in university students in Vientiane, Lao PDR. *Health Promotion International, 32*(2), 360–368. https://doi.org/10.1093/heapro/daw087

Rustagi, N., Rathore, A. S., Meena, J. K., Chugh, A., & Pal, R. (2017). Neglected health literacy undermining fluorosis control efforts: A pilot study among schoolchildren in an endemic village of rural Rajasthan, India. *Journal of Family Medicine and Primary Care, 6*(3), 533–537. https://doi.org/10.4103/2249-4863.222017

Sahoo, K. C., Tamhankar, A. J., Johansson, E., & Stålsby Lundborg, C. (2014). Community perceptions of infectious diseases, antibiotic use and antibiotic resistance in context of environmental changes: A study in Odisha, India. *Health Expectations: An International Journal of Public Participation in Health Care and Health Policy, 17*(5), 651–663. https://doi.org/10.1111/j.1369-7625.2012.00789.x

Sanders, L. M., Shaw, J. S., Guez, G., Baur, C., & Rudd, R. (2009). Health literacy and child health promotion: Implications for research, clinical care, and public policy. *Pediatrics, 124*(Suppl. 3), S306–S314. https://doi.org/10.1542/peds.2009-1162G

Savitz, S. T., Bailey, S. C., Dusetzina, S. B., Jones, W. S., Trogdon, J. G., & Stearns, S. C. (2020). Treatment selection and medication adherence for stable angina: The role of area-based health literacy. *Journal of Evaluation in Clinical*

Practice, 26(6), 1711–1721. https://doi.org/10.1111/jep.13341

Scalia, P., Durand, M.-A., Faber, M., Kremer, J. A., Song, J., & Elwyn, G. (2019). User-testing an interactive option grid decision aid for prostate cancer screening: Lessons to improve usability. *BMJ Open*, 9(5), e026748. https://doi.org/10.1136/bmjopen-2018-026748

Schaeffer, D., Gille, S., & Hurrelmann, K. (2020). Implementation of the national action plan health literacy in Germany-lessons learned. *International Journal of Environmental Research and Public Health*, 17(12). https://doi.org/10.3390/ijerph17124403

Schougaard, L. M. V., Mejdahl, C. T., Christensen, J., Lomborg, K., Maindal, H. T., de Thurah, A., & Hjollund, N. H. (2019). Patient-initiated versus fixed-interval patient-reported outcome-based follow-up in outpatients with epilepsy: A pragmatic randomized controlled trial. *Journal of Patient-Reported Outcomes*, 3(1), 61. https://doi.org/10.1186/s41687-019-0151-0

Searle, K., Blashki, G., Kakuma, R., Yang, H., Zhao, Y., & Minas, H. (2019). Current needs for the improved management of depressive disorder in community healthcare centres, Shenzhen, China: A view from primary care medical leaders. *International Journal of Mental Health Systems*, 13, 47. https://doi.org/10.1186/s13033-019-0300-0

Semakula, D., Nsangi, A., Oxman, M., Austvoll-Dahlgren, A., Rosenbaum, S., Kaseje, M., Nyirazinyoye, L., Fretheim, A., Chalmers, I., Oxman, A. D., & Sewankambo, N. K. (2017). Can an educational podcast improve the ability of parents of primary school children to assess the reliability of claims made about the benefits and harms of treatments: Study protocol for a randomised controlled trial. *Trials*, *18*(1), 31. https://doi.org/10.1186/s13063-016-1745-y

Semakula, D., Nsangi, A., Oxman, A. D., Oxman, M., Austvoll-Dahlgren, A., Rosenbaum, S., Morelli, A., Glenton, C., Lewin, S., Nyirazinyoye, L., Kaseje, M., Chalmers, I., Fretheim, A., Rose, C. J., & Sewankambo, N. K. (2020). Effects of the Informed Health Choices podcast on the ability of parents of primary school children in Uganda to assess the trustworthiness of claims about treatment effects: One-year follow up of a randomised trial. *Trials*, *21*(1), 187. https://doi.org/10.1186/s13063-020-4093-x

Seurer, A. C., & Vogt, H. B. (2013). Low health literacy: A barrier to effective patient care. *South Dakota Medicine: The Journal of the South Dakota State Medical Association*, *66*(2), 51, 53–57.

Shah, S. F. A., Ginossar, T., & Weiss, D. (2019). "This is a Pakhtun disease": Pakhtun health journalists' perceptions of the barriers and facilitators to polio vaccine acceptance among the high-risk Pakhtun community in Pakistan. *Vaccine*, *37*(28), 3694–3703. https://doi.org/10.1016/j.vaccine.2019.05.029

Shahly, V., Kessler, R. C., & Duncan, I. (2014). Worksite primary care clinics: A systematic review. *Population Health Management*, *17*(5), 306–315. https://doi.org/10.1089/pop.2013.0095

Shaikh, U., & Byrd, R. S. (2016). Population Health Considerations for Pediatric Asthma: Findings from the 2011–2012 California Health Interview Survey. *Population Health Management*, *19*(2), 145–151. https://doi.org/10.1089/pop.2015.0015

Sheon, A. R., Bolen, S. D., Callahan, B., Shick, S., & Perzynski, A. T. (2017). Addressing disparities in diabetes management through novel approaches to encourage technology adoption and use. *JMIR Diabetes*, 2(2), e16. https://doi.org/10.2196/diabetes.6751

Shlobin, N. A., Clark, J. R., Hoffman, S. C., Hopkins, B. S., Kesavabhotla, K., & Dahdaleh, N. S. (2021). Patient education in neurosurgery: Part 1 of a systematic review. *World Neurosurgery*, 147, 202–214.e1. https://doi.org/10.1016/j.wneu.2020.11.168

Siegel, C. E., Reid-Rose, L., Joseph, A. M., Hernandez, J. C., & Haugland, G. (2016). Cultural activation of consumers. *Psychiatric Services*, 67(2), 153–155. https://doi.org/10.1176/appi.ps.201500278

Slewa-Younan, S., McKenzie, M., Thomson, R., Smith, M., Mohammad, Y., & Mond, J. (2020). Improving the mental wellbeing of Arabic speaking refugees: An evaluation of a mental health promotion program. *BMC Psychiatry*, 20(1), 314. https://doi.org/10.1186/s12888-020-02732-8

Slewa-Younan, S., Nguyen, T. P., Al-Yateem, N., Rossiter, R. C., & Robb, W. (2020). Causes and risk factors for common mental illnesses: The beliefs of paediatric hospital staff in the United Arab Emirates. *International Journal of Mental Health Systems*, 14, 35. https://doi.org/10.1186/s13033-020-00367-6

Sørensen, K., Maindal, H. T., Heijmans, M., & Rademakers, J. (2020). Work in progress: A report on health literacy in Denmark and The Netherlands. *Studies in Health Technology and Informatics*, 269, 202–211. https://doi.org/10.3233/SHTI200033

St Leger, L. (2001). Schools, health literacy and public health: Possibilities and challenges. *Health Promotion International,* *16*(2), 197–205. https://doi.org/10.1093/heapro/16.2.197

Stefanacci, R. G., Reich, S., & Casiano, A. (2015). Application of PACE principles for population health management of frail older adults. *Population Health Management,* *18*(5), 367–372. https://doi.org/10.1089/pop. 2014.0096

Swahn, M. H., Braunstein, S., & Kasirye, R. (2014). Demographic and psychosocial characteristics of mobile phone ownership and usage among youth living in the Slums of Kampala, Uganda. *The Western Journal of Emergency Medicine,* *15*(5), 600–603. https://doi.org/10.5811/westjem. 2014.4.20879

Swavely, D., Whyte, V., Steiner, J. F., & Freeman, S. L. (2019). Complexities of addressing food insecurity in an urban population. *Population Health Management,* *22*(4), 300–307. https://doi.org/10.1089/pop.2018.0126

Swisher, J., Blitz, J., & Sweitzer, B. (2020). Special considerations related to race, sex, gender, and socioeconomic status in the preoperative evaluation: Part 2: Sex considerations and homeless patients. *Anesthesiology Clinics,* *38*(2), 263–278. https://doi.org/10.1016/j.anclin.2020.02.001

Tabassum, R., Froeschl, G., Cruz, J. P., Colet, P. C., Dey, S., & Islam, S. M. S. (2018). Untapped aspects of mass media campaigns for changing health behaviour towards non-communicable diseases in Bangladesh. *Globalization and Health,* *14*(1), 7. https://doi.org/10.1186/s12992-018-0325-1

Taylor, H. A., Francis, S., Evans, C. R., Harvey, M., Newton, B. A., Jones, C. P., Akintobi, T. H., & Clifford, G. (2020). Preventing cardiovascular disease among urban African

Americans with a mobile health app (the MOYO app): Protocol for a usability study. *JMIR Research Protocols*, *9*(7), e16699. https://doi.org/10.2196/16699

Taylor, D. M., Fraser, S. D. S., Bradley, J. A., Bradley, C., Draper, H., Metcalfe, W., Oniscu, G. C., Tomson, C. R. V., Ravanan, R., & Roderick, P. J. (2017). A systematic review of the prevalence and associations of limited health literacy in CKD. *Clinical Journal of the American Society of Nephrology: CJASN*, *12*(7), 1070–1084. https://doi.org/10.2215/CJN.12921216

Thomas, K., Wilson, J. L., Bedell, P., & Morse, D. S. (2019). "They didn't give up on me": A women's transitions clinic from the perspective of re-entering women. *Addiction Science & Clinical Practice*, *14*(1), 12. https://doi.org/10.1186/s13722-019-0142-8

Tiwari, T., Jamieson, L., Broughton, J., Lawrence, H. P., Batliner, T. S., Arantes, R., & Albino, J. (2018). Reducing indigenous oral health inequalities: A review from 5 nations. *Journal of Dental Research*, *97*(8), 869–877. https://doi.org/10.1177/0022034518763605

Topp, S. M., Sharma, A., Chileshe, C., Magwende, G., Henostroza, G., & Moonga, C. N. (2018). The health system accountability impact of prison health committees in Zambia. *International Journal for Equity in Health*, *17*(1), 74. https://doi.org/10.1186/s12939-018-0783-3

Tully, L. A., Hawes, D. J., Doyle, F. L., Sawyer, M. G., & Dadds, M. R. (2019). A national child mental health literacy initiative is needed to reduce childhood mental health disorders. *Australian and New Zealand Journal of Psychiatry*, *53*(4), 286–290. https://doi.org/10.1177/0004867418821440

Umubyeyi, A., Mogren, I., Ntaganira, J., & Krantz, G. (2016). Help-seeking behaviours, barriers to care and self-efficacy for seeking mental health care: A population-based study in Rwanda. *Social Psychiatry and Psychiatric Epidemiology*, *51*(1), 81–92. https://doi.org/10.1007/s00127-015-1130-2

Valaitis, R., Cleghorn, L., Ploeg, J., Risdon, C., Mangin, D., Dolovich, L., Agarwal, G., Oliver, D., Gaber, J., & Chung, H. (2020). Disconnected relationships between primary care and community-based health and social services and system navigation for older adults: A qualitative descriptive study. *BMC Family Practice*, *21*(1), 69. https://doi.org/10.1186/s12875-020-01143-8

van Koops't Jagt, R., de Winter, A. F., Reijneveld, S. A., Hoeks, J. C. J., & Jansen, C. J. M. (2016). Development of a communication intervention for older adults with limited health literacy: Photo stories to support doctor-patient communication. *Journal of Health Communication*, *21*(Suppl. 2), 69–82. https://doi.org/10.1080/10810730.2016.1193918

Vargas, C. R., Chuang, D. J., & Lee, B. T. (2014). Assessment of patient health literacy: A national survey of plastic surgeons. *Plastic and Reconstructive Surgery*, *134*(6), 1405–1414. https://doi.org/10.1097/PRS.0000000000000737

Vearey, J., Luginaah, I., Magitta, N. F., Shilla, D. J., & Oni, T. (2019). Urban health in Africa: A critical global public health priority. *BMC Public Health*, *19*(1), 340. https://doi.org/10.1186/s12889-019-6674-8

Visla, J., Shatola, A., Wisner, D. H., & Shaikh, U. (2019). Understandability and actionability of online information on hypertension. *Population Health Management*, *22*(4), 369. https://doi.org/10.1089/pop.2019.0037

Visscher, B. B., Steunenberg, B., Heerdink, E. R., & Rademakers, J. (2020). Medication self-management support for people with diabetes and low health literacy: A needs assessment. *PLoS One*, *15*(4), e0232022. https://doi.org/10.1371/journal.pone.0232022

Wahab, A., Ali, A., Nazir, S., Ochoa, L., Khan, H., Khan, M., Chaudhary, S., & Smith, S. J. (2018). A QI initiative for bridging the health literacy gap by educating internal medicine residents at a community hospital. *Journal of Community Hospital Internal Medicine Perspectives*, *8*(5), 260–266. https://doi.org/10.1080/20009666.2018.1528108

Walker, P., de Morgan, S., Sanders, D., Nicholas, M., & Blyth, F. M. (2020). Primary care initiatives focused on the secondary prevention and management of chronic pain: A scoping review of the Australian literature. *Australian Journal of Primary Health*, *26*(4), 273–280. https://doi.org/10.1071/PY20092

Wang, J., Fick, G., Adair, C., & Lai, D. (2007). Gender specific correlates of stigma toward depression in a Canadian general population sample. *Journal of Affective Disorders*, *103*(1–3), 91–97. https://doi.org/10.1016/j.jad.2007.01.010

Washington, D. M., Curtis, L. M., Waite, K., Wolf, M. S., & Paasche-Orlow, M. K. (2018). Sociodemographic factors mediate race and ethnicity-associated childhood asthma health disparities: A longitudinal analysis. *Journal of Racial and Ethnic Health Disparities*, *5*(5), 928–938. https://doi.org/10.1007/s40615-017-0441-2

Weinstein, R. S., Waer, A. L., Weinstein, J. B., Briehl, M. M., Holcomb, M. J., Erps, K. A., Holtrust, A. L., Tomkins, J. M., Barker, G. P., & Krupinski, E. A. (2017). Second Flexner Century: The democratization of medical knowledge: Repurposing a general pathology course into multigrade-level "gateway" courses. *Academic Pathology*, 4. https://doi.org/10.1177/2374289517718872

Wickramasinghe, N. (2019). Essential considerations for successful consumer health informatics solutions. *Yearbook of Medical Informatics*, 28(1), 158–164. https://doi.org/10.1055/s-0039-1677909

Wilson, C. J., Bushnell, J. A., & Caputi, P. (2011). Early access and help seeking: Practice implications and new initiatives. *Early Intervention in Psychiatry*, 5(Suppl. 1), 34–39. https://doi.org/10.1111/j.1751-7893.2010.00238.x

Wilson, J. D., Shaw, K. C., & Feldman, L. S. (2018). Using post-discharge home visitation to improve cultural sensitivity and patient-centered discharge planning by internal medicine trainees. *Journal of Health Care for the Poor and Underserved*, 29(4), 1288–1299. https://doi.org/10.1353/hpu.2018.0096

Wood, E. H., Waterman, A. D., & Pines, R. (2021). Storytelling to inspire dialysis patients to learn about living donor kidney transplant. *Blood Purification*, 50(4–5), 655–661. https://doi.org/10.1159/000512651

Wu, C.-L., Liou, C.-H., Liu, S.-A., Chen, C.-H., Sheu, W. H.-H., Chou, I.-J., & Tsai, S.-F. (2020). Quality improvement initiatives in reforming patient support groups-three-year outcomes. *International Journal of Environmental Research and Public Health*, 17(19). https://doi.org/10.3390/ijerph17197155

Yadav, L., Gill, T. K., Taylor, A., Jasper, U., de Young, J., Visvanathan, R., & Chehade, M. J. (2019). Cocreation of a digital patient health hub to enhance education and person-centred integrated care post hip fracture: A mixed-methods study protocol. *BMJ Open*, *9*(12), e033128. https://doi.org/10.1136/bmjopen-2019-033128

Yang, H.-H., Chwa, W. J., Yuen, S. B., Huynh, J. D., Chan, J. S., Kumar, A., Dhanjani, S. A., Gee, G. C., & Cowgill, B. O. (2021). APA Health CARE: A student-led initiative addressing health care barriers faced by the Asian and Pacific Islander American Immigrant Population in Los Angeles. *Journal of Community Health*, *46*(2), 367–379. https://doi.org/10.1007/s10900-020-00915-8

Yun, K., Paul, P., Subedi, P., Kuikel, L., Nguyen, G. T., & Barg, F. K. (2016). Help-seeking behavior and health care navigation by Bhutanese refugees. *Journal of Community Health*, *41*(3), 526–534. https://doi.org/10.1007/s10900-015-0126-x

Zafar, H. M., Bugos, E. K., Langlotz, C. P., & Frasso, R. (2016). "Chasing a ghost": Factors that influence primary care physicians to follow up on incidental imaging findings. *Radiology*, *281*(2), 567–573. https://doi.org/10.1148/radiol.2016152188

Zanchetta, M. S., & Poureslami, I. M. (2006). Health literacy within the reality of immigrants' culture and language. *Canadian Journal of Public Health/Revue Canadienne De Sante Publique*, *97*(Suppl. 2), S26–S30.

Zarcadoolas, C. (2011). The simplicity complex: Exploring simplified health messages in a complex world. *Health Promotion International*, *26*(3), 338–350. https://doi.org/10.1093/heapro/daq075

Zhang, J., Astell-Burt, T., Seo, D.-C., Feng, X., Kong, L., Zhao, W., Li, N., Li, Y., Yu, S., Feng, G., Ren, D., Lv, Y., Wang, J., Shi, X., Liang, X., & Chen, C. (2014). Multilevel evaluation of 'China Healthy Lifestyles for All', a nationwide initiative to promote lower intakes of salt and edible oil. *Preventive Medicine*, 67, 210–215. https://doi.org/10.1016/j.ypmed.2014.07.019

Zuckerman, K. E., Mattox, K., Donelan, K., Batbayar, O., Baghaee, A., & Bethell, C. (2013). Pediatrician identification of Latino children at risk for autism spectrum disorder. *Pediatrics*, 132(3), 445–453. https://doi.org/10.1542/peds.2013-0383

Zuercher, E., Diatta, I. D., Burnand, B., & Peytremann-Bridevaux, I. (2017). Health literacy and quality of care of patients with diabetes: A cross-sectional analysis. *Primary Care Diabetes*, 11(3), 233–240. https://doi.org/10.1016/j.pcd.2017.02.003

REFERENCES

Aaby, A., Friis, K., Christensen, B., & Maindal, H. T. (2020). Health literacy among people in cardiac rehabilitation: Associations with participation and health-related quality of life in the heart skills study in Denmark. *International Journal of Environmental Research and Public Health, 17*(2). https://doi.org/10.3390/ijerph17020443

Agency for Healthcare Research and Quality. (2020). AHRQ health literacy universal precautions toolkit. https://www.ahrq.gov/health-literacy/improve/precautions/index.html. Accessed on January 1, 2021.

Akter, S., Doran, F., Avila, C., & Nancarrow, S. (2014). A qualitative study of staff perspectives of patient non-attendance in a regional primary healthcare setting. *The Australasian Medical Journal, 7*(5), 218–226. https://doi.org/10.4066/AMJ.2014.2056

Amarasuriya, S. D., Jorm, A. F., & Reavley, N. J. (2015). Quantifying and predicting depression literacy of undergraduates: A cross sectional study in Sri Lanka. *BMC Psychiatry, 15*, 269. https://doi.org/10.1186/s12888-015-0658-8

Ammentorp, J., Bigi, S., Silverman, J., Sator, M., Gillen, P., Ryan, W., Rosenbaum, M., Chiswell, M., Doherty, E., & Martin, P. (2021). Upscaling communication skills training: Lessons learned from international initiatives. *Patient Education and Counseling, 104*(2), 352–359. https://doi.org/10.1016/j.pec.2020.08.028

Apter, A. J., Cheng, J., Small, D., Bennett, I. M., Albert, C., Fein, D. G., George, M., & van Horne, S. (2006). Asthma numeracy skill and health literacy. *Journal of Asthma: Official Journal of the Association for the Care of Asthma, 43*(9), 705–710. https://doi.org/10.1080/02770900600925585

Attygalle, U. R., Perera, H., & Jayamanne, B. D. W. (2017). Mental health literacy in adolescents: Ability to recognise problems, helpful interventions and outcomes. *Child and Adolescent Psychiatry and Mental Health, 11*, 38. https://doi.org/10.1186/s13034-017-0176-1

Bailey, S. C., Brega, A. G., Crutchfield, T. M., Elasy, T., Herr, H., Kaphingst, K., Karter, A. J., Moreland-Russell, S., Osborn, C. Y., Pignone, M., Rothman, R., & Schillinger, D. (2014). Update on health literacy and diabetes. *The Diabetes Educator, 40*(5), 581–604. https://doi.org/10.1177/0145721714540220

Baker, D. W., Gazmararian, J. A., Sudano, J., & Patterson, M. (2000). The association between age and health literacy among elderly persons. *Journals of Gerontology Series B: Psychological Sciences and Social Sciences, 55*(6), S368–S374. https://doi.org/10.1093/geronb/55.6.s368

Baker, D. W., Parker, R. M., Williams, M. V., & Clark, W. S. (1998). Health literacy and the risk of hospital admission. *Journal of General Internal Medicine, 13*(12), 791–798. https://doi.org/10.1046/j.1525-1497.1998.00242.x

Baker, D. W., Parker, R. M., Williams, M. V., Clark, W. S., & Nurss, J. (1997). The relationship of patient reading ability to self-reported health and use of health services. *American Journal of Public Health, 87*(6), 1027–1030. https://doi.org/10.2105/ajph.87.6.1027

Bala, S., Keniston, A., & Burden, M. (2020). Patient perception of plain-language medical notes generated using artificial intelligence software: Pilot mixed-methods study. *JMIR Formative Research*, 4(6), e16670. https://doi.org/10.2196/16670

Behnke, L. M., Solis, A., Shulman, S. A., & Skoufalos, A. (2013). A targeted approach to reducing overutilization: Use of percutaneous coronary intervention in stable coronary artery disease. *Population Health Management*, 16(3), 164–168. https://doi.org/10.1089/pop.2012.0019

Benis, A., Tamburis, O., Chronaki, C., & Moen, A. (2021). One digital health: A unified framework for future health ecosystems. *Journal of Medical Internet Research*, 23(2), e22189. https://doi.org/10.2196/22189

Betz, C. L., Ruccione, K., Meeske, K., Smith, K., & Chang, N. (2008). Health literacy: A pediatric nursing concern. *Pediatric Nursing*, 34(3), 231–239.

Bitzer, E. M., & Sørensen, K. (2018). Gesundheitskompetenz – Health literacy. *Das Gesundheitswesen*, 80(8–9), 754–766. https://doi.org/10.1055/a-0664-0395

Bowskill, D., & Garner, L. (2012). Medicines non-adherence: Adult literacy and implications for practice. *British Journal of Nursing*, 21(19), 1156–1159. https://doi.org/10.12968/bjon.2012.21.19.1156

Bramsved, R., Regber, S., Novak, D., Mehlig, K., Lissner, L., & Mårild, S. (2018). Parental education and family income affect birthweight, early longitudinal growth and body mass index development differently. *Acta Paediatrica*, 107(11), 1946–1952. https://doi.org/10.1111/apa.14215

Brian, R. M., & Ben-Zeev, D. (2014). Mobile health (mHealth) for mental health in Asia: Objectives, strategies, and limitations. *Asian Journal of Psychiatry*, *10*, 96–100. https://doi.org/10.1016/j.ajp.2014.04.006

Brown, J., Luderowski, A., Namusisi-Riley, J., Moore-Shelley, I., Bolton, M., & Bolton, D. (2020). Can a community-led intervention offering social support and health education improve maternal health? A repeated measures evaluation of the PACT project run in a socially deprived London borough. *International Journal of Environmental Research and Public Health*, *17*(8). https://doi.org/10.3390/ijerph17082795

Bundesgesundheitsagentur. (2015). *Empfehlungen zur Einrichtung der "Österreichischen Plattform Gesundheitskompetenz" (ÖPGK)*. Bundesministerium für Gesundheit. Accessed on September 1, 2021.

Cajita, M. I., Cajita, T. R., & Han, H. R. (2016). Health literacy and heart failure: A systematic review. *Journal of Cardiovascular Nursing*, *31*(2), 121–130. https://doi.org/10.1097/JCN.0000000000000229

Caruso, R., Magon, A., Baroni, I., Dellafiore, F., Arrigoni, C., Pittella, F., & Ausili, D. (2018). Health literacy in type 2 diabetes patients: A systematic review of systematic reviews. *Acta Diabetologica*, *55*(1), 1–12. https://doi.org/10.1007/s00592-017-1071-1

Chaudhry, S. I., Herrin, J., Phillips, C., Butler, J., Mukerjhee, S., Murillo, J., Onwuanyi, A., Seto, T. B., Spertus, J., & Krumholz, H. M. (2011). Racial disparities in health literacy and access to care among patients with heart failure. *Journal of Cardiac Failure*, *17*(2), 122–127. https://doi.org/10.1016/j.cardfail.2010.09.016

Chiarelli, L., & Edwards, P. (2006). Building healthy public policy. *Canadian Journal of Public Health/Revue Canadienne de Sante Publique*, *97*(Suppl. 2), S37–S42.

Conard, S. (2019). Best practices in digital health literacy. *International Journal of Cardiology, 292*, 277–279. https://doi.org/10.1016/j.ijcard.2019.05.070

Costa, A., Mourão, S., Santos, O., Alarcão, V., Virgolino, A., Nogueira, P., Bettencourt, M. R., Reis, S., Graça, A., & Henriques, A. (2021). I-DECIDE: A social prescribing and digital intervention protocol to promote sexual and reproductive health and quality of life among young Cape Verdeans. *International Journal of Environmental Research and Public Health, 18*(3). https://doi.org/10.3390/ijerph18030850

Coughlan, D., Sahm, L., & Byrne, S. (2012). The importance of health literacy in the development of 'self care' cards for community pharmacies in Ireland. *Pharmacy Practice, 10*(3), 143–150. https://doi.org/10.4321/s1886-36552012000300004

Crosswell, L. H. (2020). The doctor in my pocket: Examining mobile approaches to personal wellbeing. *Perspectives in Public Health, 140*(2), 93–101. https://doi.org/10.1177/1757913918823808

Cusack, L., Del Mar, C. B., Chalmers, I., Gibson, E., & Hoffmann, T. C. (2018). Educational interventions to improve people's understanding of key concepts in assessing the effects of health interventions: A systematic review. *Systematic Reviews, 7*(1), 68. https://doi.org/10.1186/s13643-018-0719-4

Dilsizian, S. E., & Siegel, E. L. (2014). Artificial intelligence in medicine and cardiac imaging: Harnessing big data and advanced computing to provide personalized medical diagnosis and treatment. *Current Cardiology Reports, 16*(1), 441. https://doi.org/10.1007/s11886-013-0441-8

Dirmaier, J., & Härter, M. (2011). Strengthening patient involvement in rehabilitation. *Bundesgesundheitsblatt – Gesundheitsforschung – Gesundheitsschutz*, *54*(4), 411–419. https://doi.org/10.1007/s00103-011-1243-z

Dowrick, C., Chew-Graham, C., Lovell, K., Lamb, J., Aseem, S., Beatty, S., Bower, P., Burroughs, H., Clarke, P., Edwards, S., Gabbay, M., Gravenhorst, K., Hammond, J., Hibbert, D., Kovandžić, M., Lloyd-Williams, M., Waheed, W., & Gask, L. (2013). Increasing equity of access to high-quality mental health services in primary care: A mixed-methods study. *Programme Grants for Applied Research*, *1*(2). NIHR Journals Library.

Dubbin, L., Burke, N., Fleming, M., Thompson-Lastad, A., Napoles, T. M., Yen, I., & Shim, J. K. (2021). Social literacy: Nurses' contribution toward the co-production of self-management. *Global Qualitative Nursing Research*, *8*. https://doi.org/10.1177/2333393621993451

Ekblad, S. (2020). To increase mental health literacy and human rights among new-coming, low-educated mothers with experience of war: A culturally, tailor-made group health promotion intervention with participatory methodology addressing indirectly the children. *Frontiers in Psychiatry*, *11*, 611. https://doi.org/10.3389/fpsyt.2020.00611

Emmerton, L. M., Mampallil, L., Kairuz, T., McKauge, L. M., & Bush, R. A. (2012). Exploring health literacy competencies in community pharmacy. *Health Expectations: An International Journal of Public Participation in Health Care and Health Policy*, *15*(1), 12–22. https://doi.org/10.1111/j.1369-7625.2010.00649.x

Eng, T. R. (2001). *The eHealth landscape. A terrain map of emerging information and communication technologies in health and heath care*. Robert Wood Johnson Foundation.

European Union. (2014a). Flash Eurobarometer 404: Eurobarometer on digital health literacy. Edited by Directorate-General for Communication. European Commission. https://data.europa.eu/data/datasets/s2020_404?locale=en. Accessed on July 20, 2021.

European Union. (2014b). Flash Eurobarometer 404 European citizens' digital health literacy: Summary. https://europa.eu/eurobarometer/api/deliverable/download/file?deliverableId=44491. Accessed on September 1, 2021.

Farokhi, M. R., Muck, A., Lozano-Pineda, J., Boone, S. L., & Worabo, H. (2018). Using interprofessional education to promote oral health literacy in a faculty-student collaborative practice. *Journal of Dental Education*, *82*(10), 1091–1097. https://doi.org/10.21815/JDE.018.110

Fathy, C., Patel, S., Sternberg, P., Jr., & Kohanim, S. (2016). Disparities in adherence to screening guidelines for diabetic retinopathy in the United States: A comprehensive review and guide for future directions. *Seminars in Ophthalmology*, *31*(4), 364–377. https://doi.org/10.3109/08820538.2016.1154170

Ferdinand, K. C., Senatore, F. F., Clayton-Jeter, H., Cryer, D. R., Lewin, J. C., Nasser, S. A., Fiuzat, M., & Califf, R. M. (2017). Improving medication adherence in cardiometabolic disease: Practical and regulatory implications. *Journal of the American College of Cardiology*, *69*(4), 437–451. https://doi.org/10.1016/j.jacc.2016.11.034

Fredrick, C. M. B., Linskens, R. J., Schilling, M. A., Eggen, A. T., Strickland, R. A., & Jacobs, E. A. (2020). The cancer clear & simple story: Developing a cancer prevention curriculum for rural Wisconsin through a community partnership. *Journal of Cancer Education: The Official Journal of the American Association for Cancer Education*. https://doi.org/10.1007/s13187-020-01819-w

Galiatsatos, P., Rios, R., Daniel Hale, W., Colburn, J. L., & Christmas, C. (2015). The lay health educator program: Evaluating the impact of this community health initiative on the medical education of resident physicians. *Journal of Religion and Health*, 54(3), 1148–1156. https://doi.org/10. 1007/s10943-015-0028-3

Garcia-Retamero, R., & Galesic, M. (2010). Who profits from visual aids: Overcoming challenges in people's understanding of risks corrected. *Social Science & Medicine*, 70(7), 1019–1025. https://doi.org/10.1016/j.socscimed.2009.11.031

Gazmararian, J. A., Williams, M. V., Peel, J., & Baker, D. W. (2003). Health literacy and knowledge of chronic disease. *Patient Education and Counseling*, 51(3), 267–275. https://doi.org/10.1016/s0738-3991(02)00239-2

Gbadamosi, S. O., Eze, C., Olawepo, J. O., Iwelunmor, J., Sarpong, D. F., Ogidi, A. G., Patel, D., Oko, J. O., Onoka, C., & Ezeanolue, E. E. (2018). A patient-held smartcard with a unique identifier and an mHealth platform to improve the availability of prenatal test results in rural Nigeria: Demonstration study. *Journal of Medical Internet Research*, 20(1), e18. https://doi.org/10.2196/jmir.8716

Goldberg, L. R., & Crocombe, L. A. (2017). Advances in medical education and practice: Role of massive open online courses. *Advances in Medical Education and Practice*, 8, 603–609. https://doi.org/10.2147/AMEP.S115321

Goldney, R. D., & Fisher, L. J. (2008). Have broad-based community and professional education programs influenced mental health literacy and treatment seeking of those with major depression and suicidal ideation? *Suicide and Life-Threatening Behavior*, 38(2), 129–142. https://doi.org/10.1521/suli.2008.38.2.129

Gómez-González, E., Gomez, E., Márquez-Rivas, J., Guerrero-Claro, M., Fernández-Lizaranzu, I., Relimpio-López, Isabel, M., Dorado, M. E., Mayorga-Buiza, M. J., Izquierdo-Ayuso, G., & Capitán-Morales, L. (2020). Artificial intelligence in medicine and healthcare: A review and classification of current and near-future applications and their ethical and social impact. http://arxiv.org/pdf/2001.09778v2

Green, J. A., Mor, M. K., Shields, A. M., Sevick, M. A., Arnold, R. M., Palevsky, P. M., Fine, M. J., & Weisbord, S. D. (2013). Associations of health literacy with dialysis adherence and health resource utilization in patients receiving maintenance hemodialysis. *American Journal of Kidney Diseases: The Official Journal of the National Kidney Foundation*, 62(1), 73–80. https://doi.org/10.1053/j.ajkd.2012.12.014

Guendelman, S., Broderick, A., Mlo, H., Gemmill, A., & Lindeman, D. (2017). Listening to communities: Mixed-method study of the engagement of disadvantaged mothers and pregnant women with digital health technologies. *Journal of Medical Internet Research*, 19(7), e240. https://doi.org/10.2196/jmir.7736

Hämeen-Anttila, K. (2016). Strategic development of medicines information: Expanding key global initiatives. *Research in Social and Administrative Pharmacy: RSAP*, 12(3), 535–540. https://doi.org/10.1016/j.sapharm.2015.07.001

Hanson, M. A., Gluckman, P. D., Ma, R. C. W., Matzen, P., & Biesma, R. G. (2012). Early life opportunities for prevention of diabetes in low and middle income countries. *BMC Public Health*, 12, 1025. https://doi.org/10.1186/1471-2458-12-1025

Harper, W., Cook, S., & Makoul, G. (2007). Teaching medical students about health literacy: 2 Chicago initiatives. *American Journal of Health Behavior*, 31(Suppl. 1). https://doi.org/10.5555/ajhb.2007.31.supp.S111

Hersh, L., Salzman, B., & Snyderman, D. (2015). Health literacy in primary care practice. *American Family Physician*, 92(2), 118–124.

Hillyer, G. C., Schmitt, K. M., Lizardo, M., Reyes, A., Bazan, M., Alvarez, M. C., Sandoval, R., Abdul, K., & Orjuela, M. A. (2017). Electronic communication channel use and health information source preferences among Latinos in Northern Manhattan. *Journal of Community Health*, 42(2), 349–357. https://doi.org/10.1007/s10900-016-0261-z

Howe, C. J., Adame, T., Lewis, B., & Wagner, T. (2020). Original research: Assessing organizational focus on health literacy in North Texas hospitals. *American Journal of Nursing*, 120(12), 24–33. https://doi.org/10.1097/01.NAJ.0000723424.47838.4d

Howley, L. (2004). *Utilizing standardized patients to enhance health literacy communication skills*. Josiah Macy Jr. Foundation.

Institute of Medicine Roundtable on Health Literacy. (2012). Ten attributes of health literate health care organisations. In C., Brach, D., Keller, L. M., Hernandez, C., Baur, R., Parker, B., Dreyer, et al. (Eds.), Institute of Medicine Roundtable on Health Literacy. https://nam.edu/wp-content/uploads/2015/06/BPH_Ten_HLit_Attributes.pdf. Accessed on July 20, 2021.

Intawong, K., Olson, D., & Chariyalertsak, S. (2021). Application technology to fight the COVID-19 pandemic: Lessons learned in Thailand. *Biochemical and Biophysical Research Communications*, 534, 830–836. https://doi.org/10.1016/j.bbrc.2020.10.097

Jessup, R. L., & Buchbinder, R. (2018). What if I cannot choose wisely? Addressing suboptimal health literacy in our patients to reduce over-diagnosis and overtreatment. *Internal Medicine Journal*, 48(9), 1154–1157. https://doi.org/10.1111/imj.14025

Johri, M., Subramanian, S. V., Sylvestre, M.-P., Dudeja, S., Chandra, D., Koné, G. K., Sharma, J. K., & Pahwa, S. (2015). Association between maternal health literacy and child vaccination in India: A cross-sectional study. *Journal of Epidemiology & Community Health*, 69(9), 849–857. https://doi.org/10.1136/jech-2014-205436

Kalichman, S. C., Benotsch, E., Suarez, T., Catz, S., Miller, J., & Rompa, D. (2000). Health literacy and health-related knowledge among persons living with HIV/AIDS. *American Journal of Preventive Medicine*, 18(4), 325–331. https://doi.org/10.1016/s0749-3797(00)00121-5

Khoong, E. C., Cherian, R., Smith, D. E., Schillinger, D., Wolf, M. S., & Sarkar, U. (2018). Implementation of patient-centered prescription labeling in a safety-net ambulatory care network. *American Journal of Health-System Pharmacy: AJHP: Official Journal of the American Society of Health-System Pharmacists*, 75(16), 1227–1238. https://doi.org/10.2146/ajhp170821

Kickbusch, I. (2021). Health literacy – Politically reloaded. *Health Promotion International*, 36(3), 601–604. https://doi.org/10.1093/heapro/daab121

Kickbusch, I., Wait, S., Maag, D., Saan, H., McGuire, P., & Banks, I. (2006). *Navigating health. The role of health literacy*. Alliance for Health and the Future, International Longevity Centre.

King, D. M., Donley, T., Mbizo, J., Higgins, M., Langaigne, A., Middleton, E. J., & Stokes-Williams, C. (2019). The use of a community-based preconception peer health educator training intervention to improve preconception health knowledge. *Journal of Racial and Ethnic Health Disparities*, 6(4), 686–700. https://doi.org/10.1007/s40615-019-00567-y

Koonrungsesomboon, N., Traivaree, C., Tiyapsane, C., & Karbwang, J. (2019). Improved parental understanding by an enhanced informed consent form: A randomized controlled study nested in a paediatric drug trial. *BMJ Open*, 9(11), e029530. https://doi.org/10.1136/bmjopen-2019-029530

Koops van't Jagt, R., de Winter, A. F., Reijneveld, S. A., Hoeks, J. C. J., & Jansen, C. J. M. (2016). Development of a communication intervention for older adults with limited health literacy: Photo stories to support doctor-patient communication. *Journal of Health Communication*, 21(Suppl. 2), 69–82. https://doi.org/10.1080/10810730.2016.1193918

Levin-Zamir, D., Sorensen, K., Su, T. T., Sentell, T., Rowlands, G., Messer, M., Pleasant, A., Saboga Nunes, L., Lev-Ari, S., & Okan, O. (2021). Health promotion preparedness for health crises – A 'must' or 'nice to have'? Case studies and global lessons learned from the COVID-19 pandemic. *Global Health Promotion*, 28(2), 27–37. https://doi.org/10.1177/1757975921998639

Levy, H., & Janke, A. (2016). Health literacy and access to care. *Journal of Health Communication*, 21(Suppl. 1), 43–50. https://doi.org/10.1080/10810730.2015.1131776

Lin, S. Y., Mahoney, M. R., & Sinsky, C. A. (2019). Ten ways artificial intelligence will transform primary care. *Journal of General Internal Medicine*, 34(8), 1626–1630. https://doi.org/10.1007/s11606-019-05035-1

Mabachi, N. M., Cifuentes, M., Barnard, J., Brega, A. G., Albright, K., Weiss, B. D., Brach, C., & West, D. (2016). Demonstration of the health literacy universal precautions toolkit: Lessons for quality improvement. *The Journal of Ambulatory Care Management, 39*(3), 199–208. https://doi.org/10.1097/JAC.0000000000000102

Maggio, L. A., Willinsky, J. M., Costello, J. A., Skinner, N. A., Martin, P. C., & Dawson, J. E. (2020). Integrating Wikipedia editing into health professions education: A curricular inventory and review of the literature. *Perspectives on Medical Education, 9*(6), 333–342. https://doi.org/10.1007/s40037-020-00620-1

Malloy-Weir, L. J., Charles, C., Gafni, A., & Entwistle, V. (2016). A review of health literacy: Definitions, interpretations, and implications for policy initiatives. *Journal of Public Health Policy, 37*(3), 334–352. https://doi.org/10.1057/jphp.2016.18

Marciano, L., Camerini, A.-L., & Schulz, P. J. (2019). The role of health literacy in diabetes knowledge, self-care, and glycemic control: A meta-analysis. *Journal of General Internal Medicine, 34*(6), 1007–1017. https://doi.org/10.1007/s11606-019-04832-y

Marshall, S., Sahm, L., & McCarthy, S. (2012). Health literacy in Ireland: Reading between the lines. *Perspectives in Public Health, 132*(1), 31–38. https://doi.org/10.1177/1757913911431034

Matima, R., Murphy, K., Levitt, N. S., BeLue, R., & Oni, T. (2018). A qualitative study on the experiences and perspectives of public sector patients in Cape Town in managing the workload of demands of HIV and type 2 diabetes multimorbidity. *PLoS One, 13*(3). https://doi.org/10.1371/journal.pone.0194191

Matsuoka, S., Tsuchihashi-Makaya, M., Kayane, T., Yamada, M., Wakabayashi, R., Kato, N. P., & Yazawa, M. (2016). Health literacy is independently associated with self-care behavior in patients with heart failure. *Patient Education and Counseling*, 99(6), 1026–1032. https://doi.org/10.1016/j.pec.2016.01.003

Mayeaux, E. J., Murphy, P. W., Arnold, C., Davis, T. C., Jackson, R. H., & Sentell, T. (1996). Improving patient education for patients with low literacy skills. *American Family Physician*, 53(1), 205–211.

McNaughton, C. D., Jacobson, T. A., & Kripalani, S. (2014). Low literacy is associated with uncontrolled blood pressure in primary care patients with hypertension and heart disease. *Patient Education and Counseling*, 96(2), 165–170. https://doi.org/10.1016/j.pec.2014.05.007

Micklethwaite, A., Brownson, C. A., O'Toole, M. L., & Kilpatrick, K. E. (2012). The business case for a diabetes self-management intervention in a community general hospital. *Population Health Management*, 15(4), 230–235. https://doi.org/10.1089/pop.2011.0051

Montagni, I., Langlois, E., Wittwer, J., & Tzourio, C. (2017). Co-creating and evaluating a web-app mapping real-world health care services for students: The servi-share protocol. *JMIR Research Protocols*, 6(2), e24. https://doi.org/10.2196/resprot.6801

Morley, J., Machado, C. C. V., Burr, C., Cowls, J., Joshi, I., Taddeo, M., & Floridi, L. (2020). The ethics of AI in health care: A mapping review. *Social Science & Medicine*, 260, 113172. https://doi.org/10.1016/j.socscimed.2020.113172

Morris, N. S., MacLean, C. D., Chew, L. D., & Littenberg, B. (2006). The single item literacy screener: Evaluation of a brief instrument to identify limited reading ability. *BMC Family Practice*, 7, 21. https://doi.org/10.1186/1471-2296-7-21

Musich, S., Wang, S. S., Kraemer, S., Hawkins, K., & Wicker, E. (2018). Purpose in life and positive health outcomes among older adults. *Population Health Management*, 21(2), 139–147. https://doi.org/10.1089/pop.2017.0063

Mwaisaka, J., Gonsalves, L., Thiongo, M., Waithaka, M., Sidha, H., Alfred, O., Mukiira, C., & Gichangi, P. (2021). Young people's experiences using an on-demand mobile health sexual and reproductive health text message intervention in Kenya: Qualitative study. *JMIR mHealth and uHealth*, 9(1), e19109. https://doi.org/10.2196/19109

Nahm, E.-S., Zhu, S., Bellantoni, M., Keldsen, L., Russomanno, V., Rietschel, M., Majid, T., Son, H., & Smith, L. (2019). The effects of a theory-based patient portal e-learning program for older adults with chronic illnesses. *Telemedicine Journal and e-Health: The Official Journal of the American Telemedicine Association*, 25(10), 940–951. https://doi.org/10.1089/tmj.2018.0184

Norman, C. D., & Skinner, H. A. (2006a). eHEALS: The eHealth literacy scale. *Journal of Medical Internet Research*, 8(4), e27. https://doi.org/10.2196/jmir.8.4.e27

Norman, C. D., & Skinner, H. A. (2006b). eHealth literacy: Essential skills for consumer health in a networked world. *Journal of Medical Internet Research*, 8(2), e9. https://doi.org/10.2196/jmir.8.2.e9

Nutbeam, D. (2000). Health literacy as a public health goal: A challenge for contemporary health education and communication strategies into the 21st century. *Health Promotion International*, 15(3), 259–267. https://doi.org/10.1093/heapro/15.3.259

Nutbeam, D. (2020). Health literacy as a public health goal: A challenge for contemporary health education and communication strategies into the 21st century. *Health Promotion International*, *15*, 259–267.

Okan, O., Bauer, U., Levin-Zamir, D., Pinheiro, P., & Sørensen, K. (Eds.). (2019). *International handbook of health literacy: Research, practice and policy across the lifespan*. Policy Press.

Palumbo, R. (2021). Leveraging organizational health literacy to enhance health promotion and risk prevention: A narrative and interpretive literature review. *Yale Journal of Biology & Medicine*, *94*(1), 115–128.

Palumbo, R., Annarumma, C., Adinolfi, P., & Musella, M. (2016). The missing link to patient engagement in Italy. *Journal of Health, Organisation and Management*, *30*(8), 1183–1203. https://doi.org/10.1108/JHOM-01-2016-0011

Parker, R. M., Baker, D. W., Williams, M. V., & Nurss, J. R. (1995). The test of functional health literacy in adults: A new instrument for measuring patients' literacy skills. *Journal of General Internal Medicine*, *10*(10), 537–541. https://doi.org/10.1007/BF02640361

Parnell, T. A., McCulloch, E. C., Mieres, J. H., & Edwards, F. (2014). Health literacy as an essential component to achieving excellent patient outcomes. *NAM Perspectives*, *4*(1). https://doi.org/10.31478/201401b

Pelikan, J. M., Ganahl, K., van den Broucke, S., & Sørensen, K. (2019). Measuring health literacy in Europe: Introducing the European health literacy survey questionnaire (HLS-EU-Q). In O. Okan, U. Bauer, D. Levin-Zamir, P. Pinheiro, & K. Sørensen (Eds.), *International handbook of health literacy: Research, practice and policy across the lifespan*. Policy Press.

Persell, S. D., Osborn, C. Y., Richard, R., Skripkauskas, S., & Wolf, M. S. (2007). Limited health literacy is a barrier to medication reconciliation in ambulatory care. *Journal of General Internal Medicine*, 22(11), 1523–1526. https://doi. org/10.1007/s11606-007-0334-x

Pinto-Meza, A., Moneta, M. V., Alonso, J., Angermeyer, M. C., Bruffaerts, R., Caldas de Almeida, J. M., Girolamo, G. de, Graaf, R. de, Florescu, S., Kovess Masfety, V., O'Neill, S., Vassilev, S., & Haro, J. M. (2013). Social inequalities in mental health: Results from the EU contribution to the world mental health surveys initiative. *Social Psychiatry and Psychiatric Epidemiology*, 48(2), 173–181. https://doi.org/10. 1007/s00127-012-0536-3

Pleasant, A., Maish, C., O'Leary, C., & Carmona, R. (2019). Measuring health literacy in adults: An overview and discussion of current tools. In O. Okan, U. Bauer, D. Levin-Zamir, P. Pinheiro, & K. Sørensen (Eds.), *International handbook of health literacy: Research, practice and policy across the lifespan*. Policy Press.

Rababah, J. A., Al-Hammouri, Mohammed, M., Drew, B. L., & Aldalaykeh, M. (2019). Health literacy: Exploring disparities among college students. *BMC Public Health*, 19(1), 1401. https://doi.org/10.1186/s12889-019-7781-2

Ratzan, S. C., & Parker, R. M. (2000). Introduction. In C. R. Selden, M. Zorn, S. C. Ratzan, & R. M. Parker (Eds.), Health Literacy, *Current Bibliographies in Medicine 2000-1*, U.S. Dept. of Health and Human Services, Public Health Service, National Institutes of Health, National Library of Medicine, Reference Section, Bethesda, 5–7.

Renzaho, A. M. N., Green, J., Smith, B. J., & Polonsky, M. (2018). Exploring factors influencing childhood obesity prevention among migrant communities in Victoria, Australia:

A qualitative study. *Journal of Immigrant and Minority Health*, *20*(4), 865–883. https://doi.org/10.1007/s10903-017-0620-6

Rezaei Aghdam, A., Watson, J., Cliff, C., & Miah, S. J. (2020). Improving the theoretical understanding toward patient-driven health care innovation through online value cocreation: Systematic review. *Journal of Medical Internet Research*, *22*(4), e16324. https://doi.org/10.2196/16324

Rogers, E. A., Fine, S., Handley, M. A., Davis, H., Kass, J., & Schillinger, D. (2014). Development and early implementation of the bigger picture, a youth-targeted public health literacy campaign to prevent type 2 diabetes. *Journal of Health Communication*, *19*(Suppl. 2), 144–160. https://doi.org/10.1080/10810730.2014.940476

Salman, R., & Weyers, S. (2010). Germany: MiMi project – With migrants for migrants. In WHO Regional Office for Europe (Ed.), *Poverty and social exclusion in the WHO European region*. Health Systems Respond.

Sanders, L. M., Shaw, J. S., Guez, G., Baur, C., & Rudd, R. (2009). Health literacy and child health promotion: Implications for research, clinical care, and public policy. *Pediatrics*, *124*(Suppl. 3), S306–S314. https://doi.org/10.1542/peds.2009-1162G

Schillinger, D., Bindman, A., Wang, F., Stewart, A., & Piette, J. (2004). Functional health literacy and the quality of physician–Patient communication among diabetes patients. *Patient Education and Counseling*, *52*(3), 315–323. https://doi.org/10.1016/S0738-3991(03)00107-1

Schillinger, D., Grumbach, K., Piette, J., Wang, F., Osmond, D., Daher, C., Palacios, J., Sullivan, G. D., & Bindman, A. B. (2002). Association of health literacy with diabetes outcomes. *JAMA*, *288*(4), 475–482. https://doi.org/10.1001/jama.288.4.475

Scott, T. L., Gazmararian, J. A., Williams, M. V., & Baker, D. W. (2002). Health literacy and preventive health care use among medicare enrollees in a managed care organization. *Medical Care*, 40(5), 395–404. https://doi.org/10.1097/00005650-200205000-00005

Scovino, C. (2021). Health literacy tra prevenzione e processo di cura. https://www.nurse24.it/dossier/salute/health-literacy-prevenzione-processo-cura.html

Semakula, D., Nsangi, A., Oxman, M., Austvoll-Dahlgren, A., Rosenbaum, S., Kaseje, M., Nyirazinyoye, L., Fretheim, A., Chalmers, I., Oxman, A. D., & Sewankambo, N. K. (2017). Can an educational podcast improve the ability of parents of primary school children to assess the reliability of claims made about the benefits and harms of treatments: Study protocol for a randomised controlled trial. *Trials*, 18(1), 31. https://doi.org/10.1186/s13063-016-1745-y

Semakula, D., Nsangi, A., Oxman, A. D., Oxman, M., Austvoll-Dahlgren, A., Rosenbaum, S., Morelli, A., Glenton, C., Lewin, S., Nyirazinyoye, L., Kaseje, M., Chalmers, I., Fretheim, A., Rose, C. J., & Sewankambo, N. K. (2020). Effects of the informed health choices podcast on the ability of parents of primary school children in Uganda to assess the trustworthiness of claims about treatment effects: One-year follow up of a randomised trial. *Trials*, 21(1), 187. https://doi.org/10.1186/s13063-020-4093-x

Sentell, T. (2012). Implications for reform: Survey of California adults suggests low health literacy predicts likelihood of being uninsured. *Health Affairs*, 31(5), 1039–1048. https://doi.org/10.1377/hlthaff.2011.0954

Shah, S. F. A., Ginossar, T., & Weiss, D. (2019). "This is a Pakhtun disease": Pakhtun health journalists' perceptions of the barriers and facilitators to polio vaccine acceptance among the high-risk Pakhtun community in Pakistan. *Vaccine*, 37(28), 3694–3703. https://doi.org/10.1016/j.vaccine.2019.05.029

Simonds, S. K. (1974). Health education as social policy. *Health Education Monographs*, 2(1 Suppl), 1–10. https://doi. org/10.1177/10901981740020S102

Slewa-Younan, S., McKenzie, M., Thomson, R., Smith, M., Mohammad, Y., & Mond, J. (2020). Improving the mental wellbeing of Arabic speaking refugees: An evaluation of a mental health promotion program. *BMC Psychiatry*, 20(1), 314. https://doi.org/10.1186/s12888-020-02732-8

Smith, B., & Magnani, J. W. (2019). New technologies, new disparities: The intersection of electronic health and digital health literacy. *International Journal of Cardiology*, 292, 280–282. https://doi.org/10.1016/j.ijcard.2019.05.066

Sørensen, K., Pelikan, J. M., Röthlin, F., Ganahl, K., Slonska, Z., Doyle, G., Fullam, J., Kondilis, B., Agrafiotis, D., Uiters, E., Falcon, M., Mensing, M., Tchamov, K., van den Broucke, S., & Brand, H. (2015). Health literacy in Europe: Comparative results of the European health literacy survey (HLS-EU). *The European Journal of Public Health*, 25(6), 1053–1058. https:// doi.org/10.1093/eurpub/ckv043

Sørensen, K., van den Broucke, S., Fullam, J., Doyle, G., Pelikan, J., Slonska, Z., & Brand, H. (2012). Health literacy and public health: A systematic review and integration of definitions and models. *BMC Public Health*, 12, 80. https:// doi.org/10.1186/1471-2458-12-80

St Leger, L. (2001). Schools, health literacy and public health: Possibilities and challenges. *Health Promotion International*, 16(2), 197–205. https://doi.org/10.1093/heapro/16.2.197

Swahn, M. H., Braunstein, S., & Kasirye, R. (2014). Demographic and psychosocial characteristics of mobile phone ownership and usage among youth living in the slums of Kampala, Uganda. *Western Journal of Emergency*

Medicine, 15(5), 600–603. https://doi.org/10.5811/westjem.2014.4.20879

Tabassum, R., Froeschl, G., Cruz, J. P., Colet, P. C., Dey, S., & Islam, S. M. S. (2018). Untapped aspects of mass media campaigns for changing health behaviour towards non-communicable diseases in Bangladesh. *Globalization and Health, 14*(1), 7. https://doi.org/10.1186/s12992-018-0325-1

Taylor, H. A., Francis, S., Evans, C. R., Harvey, M., Newton, B. A., Jones, C. P., Akintobi, T. H., & Clifford, G. (2020). Preventing cardiovascular disease among urban African Americans with a mobile health app (the MOYO app): Protocol for a usability study. *JMIR Research Protocols, 9*(7), e16699. https://doi.org/10.2196/16699

Thomas, K., Wilson, J. L., Bedell, P., & Morse, D. S. (2019). "They didn't give up on me": A women's transitions clinic from the perspective of re-entering women. *Addiction Science & Clinical Practice, 14*(1), 12. https://doi.org/10.1186/s13722-019-0142-8

Umubyeyi, A., Mogren, I., Ntaganira, J., & Krantz, G. (2016). Help-seeking behaviours, barriers to care and self-efficacy for seeking mental health care: A population-based study in Rwanda. *Social Psychiatry and Psychiatric Epidemiology, 51*(1), 81–92. https://doi.org/10.1007/s00127-015-1130-2

van den Broucke, S. (2020). Why health promotion matters to the COVID-19 pandemic, and vice versa. *Health Promotion International, 35*(2), 181–186. https://doi.org/10.1093/heapro/daaa042

Vargas, C. R., Chuang, D. J., & Lee, B. T. (2014). Assessment of patient health literacy: A national survey of plastic surgeons. *Plastic and Reconstructive Surgery, 134*(6), 1405–1414. https://doi.org/10.1097/PRS.0000000000000737

Walker, P., de Morgan, S., Sanders, D., Nicholas, M., & Blyth, F. M. (2020). Primary care initiatives focused on the secondary prevention and management of chronic pain: A scoping review of the Australian literature. *Australian Journal of Primary Health*, 26(4), 273–280. https://doi.org/10.1071/PY20092

Wang, J. L., Fick, G., Adair, C., & Lai, D. (2007). Gender specific correlates of stigma toward depression in a Canadian general population sample. *Journal of Affective Disorders*, 103(1–3), 91–97. https://doi.org/10.1016/j.jad.2007.01.010

Washington, D. M., Curtis, L. M., Waite, K., Wolf, M. S., & Paasche-Orlow, M. K. (2018). Sociodemographic factors mediate race and ethnicity-associated childhood asthma health disparities: A longitudinal analysis. *Journal of Racial and Ethnic Health Disparities*, 5(5), 928–938. https://doi.org/10.1007/s40615-017-0441-2

Weinstein, R. S., Waer, A. L., Weinstein, J. B., Briehl, M. M., Holcomb, M. J., Erps, K. A., Holtrust, A. L., Tomkins, J. M., Barker, G. P., & Krupinski, E. A. (2017). Second flexner century: The democratization of medical knowledge: Repurposing a general pathology course into multigrade-level "gateway" courses. *Academic Pathology*, 4. https://doi.org/10.1177/2374289517718872

WHO Health Evidence Network. (2019). *What is the evidence on the methods, frameworks and indicators used to evaluate health literacy policies, programmes and interventions at the regional, national and organizational levels?* WHO Health Evidence Network Synthesis Report 65. World Health Organization. Regional Office for Europe. Health Evidence Network Synthesis Report, 65. https://apps.who.int/iris/handle/10665/326901. Accessed on September 1, 2021.

Williams, M. V., Baker, D. W., Honig, E. G., Lee, T. M., & Nowlan, A. (1998a). Inadequate literacy is a barrier to asthma knowledge and self-care. *Chest, 114*(4), 1008–1015. https://doi.org/10.1378/chest.114.4.1008

Williams, M. V., Baker, D. W., Parker, R. M., & Nurss, J. R. (1998b). Relationship of functional health literacy to patients' knowledge of their chronic disease: A study of patients with hypertension and diabetes. *Archives of Internal Medicine, 158*(2), 166–172. https://doi.org/10.1001/archinte.158.2.166

Williams, M. V., Parker, R. M., Baker, D. W., Parikh, N. S., Pitkin, K., Coates, W. C., & Nurss, J. R. (1995). Inadequate functional health literacy among patients at two public hospitals. *JAMA, 274*(21), 1677–1682.

Wilson, J. D., Shaw, K. C., & Feldman, L. S. (2018). Using post-discharge home visitation to improve cultural sensitivity and patient-centered discharge planning by internal medicine trainees. *Journal of Health Care for the Poor and Underserved, 29*(4), 1288–1299. https://doi.org/10.1353/hpu.2018.0096

WHO. (2013). *Health literacy: The solid facts.* In I., Kickbusch, J., Pelikan, F., Apfel, & A. D., Tsouros (Eds.), World Health Organization. http://gbv.eblib.com/patron/FullRecord.aspx?p=1582975

Wolf, M. S., Gazmararian, J. A., & Baker, D. W. (2005). Health literacy and functional health status among older adults. *Archives of Internal Medicine, 165*(17), 1946–1952. https://doi.org/10.1001/archinte.165.17.1946

Wu, C.-L., Liou, C.-H., Liu, S.-A., Chen, C.-H., Sheu, W. H.-H., Chou, I.-J., & Tsai, S.-F. (2020). Quality improvement initiatives in reforming patient support groups-three-year outcomes. *International Journal of Environmental Research and Public Health, 17*(19). https://doi.org/10.3390/ijerph17197155

Yang, H.-H., Chwa, W. J., Yuen, S. B., Huynh, J. D., Chan, J. S., Kumar, A., Dhanjani, S. A., Gee, G. C., & Cowgill, B. O. (2021). APA Health CARE: A student-led initiative addressing health care barriers faced by the Asian and Pacific Islander American Immigrant Population in Los Angeles. *Journal of Community Health*, 46(2), 367–379. https://doi.org/10.1007/s10900-020-00915-8

Zanchetta, M. S., & Poureslami, I. M. (2006). Health literacy within the reality of immigrants' culture and language. *Canadian Journal of Public Health/Revue Canadienne de Sante Publique*, 97(Suppl. 2), S26–S30.

INDEX

Printed in the United States
by Baker & Taylor Publisher Services